Jack K
June 18, 1955

Otho Winger in His Mature Strength

Otho Winger

1877 - 1946

by

V. F. Schwalm
President of Manchester College

BRETHREN PUBLISHING HOUSE
ELGIN, ILLINOIS

Printed in the United States of America

DEDICATION

*To Florence,
my faithful wife and
gracious companion*

Contents

	Page
Preface	9
Early Years and Education	15
Otho Winger as a Teacher	38
Otho Winger as the Builder of a College	51
Otho Winger as a Churchman	108
His Role in the Church of the Brethren	165
Otho Winger as a Traveler	186
His Writings and Other Interests	209
His Devotion to His Family	227
Personal Qualities of President Winger	243
Toward the Sunset	267
A Crowned Life	273
Notes from President Winger's Diary	284

Preface

Long before Otho Winger died many people felt that someone should write the story of his life. He was a colorful character who had played an important role in the fields of religion and education. He had achieved great success and represented in his person a number of unique qualities. It seemed right that someone should write the history of his achievements and portray his personality.

It was the hope of his younger brother, J. Oscar, who was usually called "J. O.," that he might be able to undertake the study and write the story. He had, however, already been suffering for some time from the illness which led to his death. After some attempts at writing, J. O. discovered that he could not carry out the plan. The confinement, the sustained application, and the emotional strain required to carry out the task were more than he could bear.

I had expressed a concern that someone write the story. When the sons, Robert and Paul, learned that J. O. could not undertake the task, they came to me asking whether I would care to attempt it. Though busy with college and church activities, I agreed to attempt the work with the provision that I should not be forced to rush hastily into print. There was much available source material to examine before writing. The accomplishment has been delayed more than I had anticipated because of a financial campaign at the college and for other reasons.

In preparing the story it has been my purpose to present Otho Winger as he was. The Germans have an expression, first extensively used by von Ranke, the great historian, "Wie es eigentlich gewesen" (as it actually was), which expresses my purpose. President Winger was an interesting person, alert, active and powerful, and individualistic. If people could see him as he actually was the story would be interesting. For that reason I have quoted extensively from his own words, as found in his diaries, letters, and other writings.

In order not to seem technical and not to make reading more difficult, I have rarely used footnotes and references. The quotations and the facts can, however, be verified if necessary. I cannot hope to have succeeded entirely in my purpose of presenting the real Otho Winger, for, as he taught me many years ago, "words half conceal and half reveal the truth" they would convey; but if something of his living personality shines through these pages I shall be pleased.

The sources of the study are many and varied. The most fruitful are (1) his thousands of letters to and from all sorts of people, (2) his diary extending through a period of about twenty-five years, (3) the full reports of the Annual Conference of the Church of the Brethren from 1907 to 1927—the most active period of his life, (4) his book, *Memories of Manchester,* an account of his work as college president and much other interesting data about his life, (5) his booklet, *In Memory of Ida Miller Winger,* containing much valuable biographical material, (6) the diary and notebooks left by Mrs. Winger telling of their trip around the world and other travels, (7) the trustee and faculty meeting minutes, (8) his annual reports to the trustees, (9) his articles in the *Gospel Messenger* through a period of thirty or more years, (10) his book, *Letters from Foreign Lands,* telling of his trip around the world, and (11) the various publications of the college during the period of his presidency.

It was also my great privilege to have been closely associated with President Winger, as student, colleague, and personal friend for nearly forty years—first as student, then as a teacher in his faculty, then as the dean for ten years, and for about eight years as a member of the executive board of the college. After that we were fellow college presidents with constant correspondence for fourteen years. From 1941, when I became his successor at Manchester, until his death, I visited him frequently.

It is more than I could hope to do to be able to write an entirely unbiased, objective story of the life of one with whom I had been so intimately associated and who has meant so much in my life. How near I have come to presenting the true story of his life, the reader will judge.

I am indebted to his sons, Robert and Paul, for the privilege of knowing their father even better than I had ever known him in life, by their making available to me his intimate papers, and to many others who have contributed to make the study possible.

PREFACE

The entire manuscript has been read by R. H. Miller, professor of religion and philosophy at Manchester College, who also knew President Winger through many years; by William M. Beahm, dean of Bethany Biblical Seminary; by Paul and Robert Winger, sons of President Winger; by Kermit Eby of the Chicago University faculty; and by Dr. L. M. Hoff of Manchester College. Mrs. Schwalm listened patiently through the reading of many sections of the manuscript and made helpful suggestions at many points.

V. F. Schwalm
Manchester College
North Manchester, Indiana

Otho Winger

Early Years and Education

Otho Winger was born on a farm near Somerset, Grant County, Indiana, on October 23, 1877. He was the son of John Martin and Mary Smith Winger, both of whom were natives of Grant County, of which Marion is the county seat.

Father Winger was a man of rugged physical strength and of determination, a man who had a lively sense of humor and enjoyed a practical joke. He liked folks and enjoyed being with neighbors in friendly jest and conversation.

Otho's mother was a pioneer mother of unusual physical strength and energy, a sincere Christian deeply devoted to her church and to her family. She belonged to that group of frontier mothers who became skilled practical nurses to the whole community. Often when caring for neighbors with contagious diseases she returned to her home at midnight, disinfected her clothing and then joined her own family. She was greatly devoted to her children and they responded to her love with life-long loyalty and affection. Her influence over the entire family was profound.

In late years Father and Mother Winger moved to North Manchester, within a half-block of Otho's home, and here they both died, the father on June 5, 1922, and the mother on October 23, 1933. Otho was always very thoughtful of his parents. He often took them with him on his preaching journeys, especially when he went back to their old home community to funerals and for other special occasions. His diary tells occasionally about having "had a good long talk with Father this evening." His mother lived eleven years after the father's passing and during much of this time she was not in good health because of repeated occurrence of skin cancer. During this time she was the object of the solicitous concern of her son Otho and others of the family. His diary reflects the most tender sentiments concerning the passing of his parents.

There were nine children in the Winger family: Otho, Bertie, Elizabeth, Ethel, J. Oscar, Cora, Mabel, Mary Florence, and John Lawrence. Bertie and Mary Florence died in infancy. The others grew to maturity and have taken their places as useful members of the church and society.

Otho was the oldest child of the family. His early boyhood was that of the usual country lad with a strong healthy body, plenty of energy, and an active mind. Along with usual boyhood activities he loved especially to swim and spent no little time at the "old swimmin' hole" near his home. He went to the neighborhood rural school called Cart Creek. The testimony of his sisters is that he loved to read, and very early in his life his mother assigned him a special room on the second floor of the home where he did his reading. Here he often stayed up until very late at night with his reading and studying.

He joined the Church of the Brethren, of which his parents were members, when he was ten years

of age. Always afterwards he was active and interested in attending and participating in the work of
the Sunday school and the church. The family was
large, and Otho, being the eldest, often helped his
mother care for the younger children. Once when
he and his mother with the younger children attended meetings at Mexico, Indiana, someone seeing
him so concerned with the welfare of the children
mistook him for the father.

All who knew Otho Winger, the man, will be
interested to know that when he was just a lad he
began his lifelong habit of visiting the sick. A neighbor reported that when one of her own family was
sick with typhoid fever, Otho came to see the sick
person every evening. Others who knew him have
borne similar testimony. His innate love of people,
his sympathy for the sick or unfortunate, and the
example of his parents likely account for this quality in his life. Both parents were greatly interested
in the sick and the unfortunate. This was especially
true of the mother.

As always happens in homes where there are
boys who feel their growing strength, there was in
the Winger home much tussling and wrestling.
J. Oscar was thirteen and a half years younger
than Otho, but as he began to grow larger and
stronger he occasionally challenged Otho to a wrestling bout. Once when Otho was at home during a
vacation period and was preaching nightly at the
home church, Oscar came to the house and taunted
him with a challenge to a wrestling match. So Otho
"took him on" and in the match threw Oscar in such
a way as to break his collarbone. It is needless to

17

say that this embarrassed Otho very greatly; that evening the sermon at the church was very short.

At another time, Otho picked J. Oscar up and threw him into the water tank, forgetting for the time that a water pipe projected a few inches into the tank. Oscar received a cut which left a scar as a lifelong reminder of these youthful pranks. This too was an object of regret to the older brother. These are but a few of the mishaps in a series of friendly skirmishes such as usually occur in families of boys.

Sometime in his early teens, Otho planned to go to Mount Morris College in Illinois, which was quite well known in Indiana. Unfortunately, during the summer his father was injured on the farm and had to spend part of a year in the hospital. As a result of this injury, the father lost his health. So, for Otho, college had to be given up because he found it necessary to help with the work on the farm. In 1895 he went to Annual Conference at Decatur, Illinois. Here he met the veteran educator, J. G. Royer, and some of his students and teachers and received added inspiration to attend college.

At the Decatur meeting he also met Reverend L. T. Holsinger, who was active in promoting the founding of a college at North Manchester, Indiana. Mr. Holsinger seems to have inspired Otho with his friendliness. During the summer, Elder David Hollinger also came to the Winger home to raise money for Manchester College, and Father Winger, true to his usually generous nature, gave him some help, though he was not sure that any of his family would attend college.

During the summer, though without a day of high school or normal work, Otho took and passed the examination for a teacher's license. That fall he was given a school by a friend of the family, James Anthony, though there were fifty-four candidates for fourteen positions. Otho was assigned the Indian Village school, one of those precarious jobs of which there were many in those days, where teachers stayed only one year. It seems that the people of Indian Village and Otho Winger, however, soon became friends, for he remained there for three years. His lifelong interest in Indians, which late in life became an absorbing hobby, likely was awakened during these early years.

The desire for college would not down in this eager, energetic young man. In the winter of 1898 he made a visit to Manchester College during a Bible institute. Here he heard singing that interested and charmed him, and preaching by the rugged and vigorous preacher, J. C. Murray, which impressed him. On this visit he was entertained in the home of John Miller and family. He became a good friend of the family and twenty-five years later when Mr. Miller died at the age of ninety Otho preached his funeral.

In the spring of 1898 he came to North Manchester to do some trading. He tells the following story in his *Memories of Manchester*. I shall let him tell it in his own words for both the story and his telling of it are characteristic of him.

I went to the Lawrence clothing store where Rev. A. L. Wright was one of the clerks. I purchased a suit of clothes and then Rev. Wright proposed that I should buy an overcoat, saying that they were selling at that time for much less than they would be in the fall. So I purchased one. Then I went to the college and got very much interested in the college bookstore where I purchased a number of books. I did not notice that my money was getting low until I looked at my change and found I had 56 cents left. It would cost me 40 cents to buy my ticket back to Lafontaine and I owed 25 cents there at the livery barn where I had left the horse and buggy for the day. Though I was a stranger I might have borrowed a quarter to save myself any difficulty, but I thought I could do it another way. I had about two hours until train time, so I packed the new clothing I had purchased and the books and started down the railroad track for Urbana. I walked that distance of six or seven miles, beat the passenger train to the station, purchased my ticket, and saved 10 cents by walking that distance. When I reached Lafontaine I had money to pay for the keep of my horse that day and had 1 cent left. That I contributed to the Sunday School the next day. I mention this because my friend, Billings, used to tell the story in the News Journal. This is the basis of the story which he printed.

Mr. Billings was the editor of the *News Journal* of North Manchester.

In September of 1898, Otho Winger found himself at Manchester College as a student. His roommate was Asa Miller, from his own home community. They, along with six other boys, roomed in the home of David Hollinger and wife. Though both Otho and Asa had taught school they were unfamiliar with college ways and had much to learn.

Manchester was really not a college then in the present accepted sense. Very few of the students had finished high school. Most of them were in the Bible school, the academy, the normal school, or the music school, or were taking some elementary commercial work. In the year 1897-1898 there were only four students listed in the collegiate department, out of a total of three hundred thirty-one students. One hundred fifty-two of these were Bible school students, while the rest were classified as follows: (a) teachers and academic department, one hundred forty-three; (b) the commercial department, forty-seven; (c) the shorthand department, sixteen; (d) the music department, fifty-seven.

Let us look at the background of this young man as he entered Manchester College. From early youth he had been deeply religious. He became a member of the church when he was ten years of age and had been baptized by Elder J. F. Spitzer, a local evangelist of that day. He had been active in the work of the Sunday school and the church as a boy and a young man. In 1896 he had been elected to the office of deacon in his home church, Cart Creek. On April 9, 1897, when he was only nineteen and one-half years old, he was licensed to preach. He preached his first sermon on April 19, ten days later, from Exodus 3:13, "What shall I say unto the people?" He was entrusted with additional responsibilities in the church two years later. (We Brethren say he was advanced to the second degree of the ministry.) On November 12, 1910, he was ordained to the eldership, the highest ministerial office in the church, by the laying on of hands. The officiating minister on this occasion was Daniel Snell, a man of considerable strength and influence in his day.

Let us try to visualize Otho Winger as he entered Manchester College in 1898. He was now nearly twenty-one years of age. As the oldest son of a large farm family, the father of which had lost his health, he had carried responsibility which helped mature him. Physically he was about five feet nine or ten inches in height. His pictures of this time show him large framed and broad shouldered, but not heavy set as later. He had a large well-shaped head and a rather round face with a strong, firmly set lower jaw. He had plenty of stubborn dark brown hair. He had what seemed like boundless energy and great physical strength. He came to college dressed in the plain garb of a Brethren minister. Alice Ebey says that he came to college with a red bandanna handkerchief around his neck. His clothing, while substantial and adequate, was not then or ever a matter of primary concern to him. In fact, a story—probably apocryphal — is told of him going to literary society once in a hurry, only to arrive wearing one tan shoe and one black shoe. Another current story is that he went to see his fiancée wearing one tan and one black shoe. He had a buoyant spirit and a brilliant, curious, and retentive mind. He had taught school for three years and had done some preaching. His equipment and experience as a preparation for college were far beyond that of the average boy or girl who came just out of high school.

Already at this time he was interested in talking to older people who had experience and insight. When a young man he often went to the home of Stephen Ulrey, a wise old elder of the church living four or five miles south of North Manchester. He would sit and talk with him about the problems of the church and of religion. Stephen Ulrey had a houseful of children of his own, but Otho Winger's interest was in conversation with Father Ulrey.

Though Otho had now taught school for three years, he had had no formal high school training. He plunged into his academy course and took it at a rapid rate. During this time he was active in the Bible Society and soon came to be one of its leading members. His vigorous personality and genial spirit made him a strong leader in the whole student body.

The college was in a precarious condition during his days as a student. Four presidents presided in as many years. The resources of the college were meager. The faculty was not strong, and the students were few. For a while matters became so serious that it seemed the college might have to close. Then Elder I. D. Parker of Elkhart, Indiana, a veteran minister and friend of education, offered to go out and attempt to raise funds to save the college. Thirty thousand dollars would be required. So during that year, 1901, Otho Winger offered his services to go out into the field and help raise funds to save the school he had chosen to attend. He tramped on foot from house to house through winter snows for some weeks to gather funds (never more than ten dollars) from plain country people in a day when higher education was not popular in the Church of the Brethren. And thus began a long series of services for "his" college—a labor of love which was to continue through nearly forty years. One cannot refrain from wondering what would have happened if this young man had followed his earlier inclination to attend Mount Morris College, rather than Manchester College. Perhaps, then, Manchester and Mount Morris might have merged at Mount Morris rather than at North Manchester.

Thanks to Reverend I. D. Parker, Otho Winger, and others, the thirty thousand dollars was raised and the cloud was lifted. The college went on its way to a greater future.

After this interval, Otho Winger returned to college, for he had planned to continue his studies at Manchester. But there were only six collegiate students enrolled that year, and only three in the freshman class: George Hamilton, Noble Stutsman, and Otho Winger. In a class meeting, George Hamilton was elected president, Noble Stutsman secretary, and Otho Winger treasurer. Soon George Hamilton secured a Rhodes scholarship to attend Oxford University and Noble Stutsman secured a job and went to work; so Otho Winger decided to leave Manchester and attend Indiana University.

Before coming to college he apparently had given considerable evidence of more than casual interest in those of the opposite sex. In college this interest continued. There were uncertainty and some wavering and changes before his affections finally settled on the teacher of shorthand and typing at Manchester College, Miss Ida Miller. Miss Miller was the daughter of Mr. and Mrs. Amos Miller, well-to-do farmers of near North Manchester. She was a tall, attractive, and dignified young woman with good training, good bearing, and good character. She was serious minded and deeply religious.

These young people really discovered each

other only about a year before their marriage, but that year they were much together. Their friendship developed into an ardent, all-absorbing love. Each one seemed the complete fulfillment of the other's need for companionship and affection. Their letters reveal all the ardor of those of Robert and Elizabeth Barrett Browning, lacking only their lyrical quality—though some are interspersed with poetry and a few become poetic prose. The week before his marriage, in a thirty-page letter he wrote to Ida: "I went down to the gaswell derrick the other day and climbed to its summit—to the height of the tree tops. I gazed in all directions but especially to the north, toward the dwelling of my beloved. Happy thoughts."

Summing up their experiences during their courtship, Otho wrote, the week before their wedding:

As to our feelings and experiences during the past year no tongue can express. Our relations with one another have been most enjoyable. . . . Never once has there been that that could cause us to doubt that true love was moving our hearts, nor that we were not admirably suited for each other's companionship. In spirit and in thought we have lived together for a year. We have exchanged through the mail our best thoughts. Together we have discussed high ideals of life. We have looked at life in its sterner realities nor shall we enter upon its duties dreaming only of flowery beds of ease. Together we have delved into some of the Masterpieces of Literature. We have walked before men together in such a way that not one can testify truthfully of a single imprudent act from us in society. We have roamed over hill and dale enjoying the beauties of nature together. We have entered into the family circle and have played no little part there. We have spent hours, days, and weeks, may I say in each other's presence only loving each other and learning more of our suitability. Truest love, devotion, and confidence have caused us to fully unfold to the other the secrets of our lives and beings as few lovers do. At no time has our love been strained. It has been natural, free, and wholesouled.

In one of these letters, referring to their approaching marriage, Otho wrote:

I shall enter the new life with joy and high hopes and ambitions. With a faith in God and a belief that I have a mission in the world, I shall launch out on life's sea with desires to aid humanity and when my days of preparation are over I hope to be able to stand in the thickest of life's conflict where duties and responsibilities are many and great and where opportunities for achievement and victories are many. . . . With you by my side I'll gladly meet whatever comes, be it prosperity or adversity and by the aid of your devoted woman's heart and the strong arm of God to aid and direct (I) we shall conquer in the End.

These two were married at six o'clock in the evening of July 24, 1902, at the bride's home about two miles west of North Manchester. Reverend A. L. Wright performed the ceremony. The story of the wedding and the honeymoon that followed is beautifully told in the twenty-two-page essay found among Otho Winger's papers. The essay is entitled *Our Wedding Tour*, and seems to be in Mrs. Winger's handwriting, though at times it seems like Mr. Winger speaking. They say, "The ceremony at this time was but the natural climax of the associations of the two, who long before the wedding day had united in heart and fortune for weal or woe, if it be for weal, they would share its joys; if woe, they would meet life's stern realities bravely."

After the wedding came the wedding dinner. Then the "giving of gifts to the bridal pair, and saying happy goodnights. But not all was quiet for the night. For at an unexpected moment there burst in wild discord. Dynamite and circular saws lent their discordant noises to increase the music. The youthful party was then invited in, and after they extended congratulations they were treated to pie and cake."

The next day they visited the groom's parental home. "Here new relatives and customs awaited. These to a great degree were to determine her future happiness. But she was received with great delight and welcomed to freely share alike the simple comforts of the new home with the older members of the family." So Mrs. Winger tells the story.

On Saturday, July 26, the bride and the groom left for a honeymoon trip to Niagara Falls. They left Marion by train on Saturday evening for Toledo, Ohio, and took a boat that night for Cleveland. They spent Sunday at Cleveland, and then took a boat to Buffalo. From here they went by street-car to Niagara Falls and put up at the Niagara Falls Hotel. Then for three or four days they remained here and saw the falls from every vantage point, took a ride on the Maid of the Mist below the falls, visited the Cave of the Winds, and one day went to Toronto and back.

These descriptions in the essay are impressive and certain general remarks are revealing as to the character and mood of the newlyweds. In Cleveland they were impressed with the growing commercial city, the wide streets and the monuments to J. D. Rockefeller and James A. Garfield. Of the tomb of Garfield they say:

Just beneath the dome where one enters the memorial is a statue of Garfield, a little larger than life-size. It shows him delivering one of his earnest and eloquent addresses to his fellow countrymen whom he sought to serve with ardent zeal. And so natural does it seem that one can almost imagine that he sees the twinkle of his eye and the blood coursing through the veins of his majestic temples and brow, and would fain listen for some word from the expressive lips. Descending a flight of stairs the visitor sees the casket that contains the mortal remains of the beloved president and nearby are those of his faithful and proud mother to whom he owed much of his greatness. There their ashes await the sound of Gabriel's trumpet that shall call the sleeping millions from their dusty beds to meet the Lord in judgment.

· · · · ·

Awakening a little before day and again going out on deck, we found the watchman wrapped in his seaman's coat and standing at the stern of the vessel assisting the pilot locate safe and dangerous places. And there we thought of the many toiling ones into whose care we commit our safety on land and sea. Heroes they are though their names are unknown; yet they follow faithfully that royal banner of true manhood and womanhood—Duty.

It is interesting that bound in the same notebook as the story of the honeymoon is a carefully typed essay on "Duty" by Otho Winger which appeared in the *Gospel Messenger* soon thereafter.

At Buffalo they visited President McKinley's home, in which he had recently died.

The home is not showy but presents a majestic appearance. In the northeast room of the second story lay the victim of the assassin's bullet. In here as the morning sun kissed the flowers and trees it could also shine and bring a ray of gladness to the dying man. Here was centered a nation's interests as the people watched and waited and prayed for more cheering news from their beloved chieftain. Here were spoken his last words as a solace to his country's children, words which will ever be cherished in every true American heart:

"It is God's will; His will be done."

Here are a few sentences of description of various scenes at the falls:

Our next view was from Prospect Point where right at our feet that mighty volume of water takes its wild leap into the chasm below. To describe one's own feeling as he stands here is well nigh impossible. Awe, admiration, and delight are intermingled and the visitor looks and looks again and walks in speechless musings.

To see the mighty volume of water dashing toward the whirlpool with terrible speed and piling itself into waves forty and fifty feet high, defying man to venture to molest its playful work is a sight never to be forgotten by him who sees and ponders over the mighty works of God.

The essay ends with these lines: "Truly, indeed, we were thankful to Our Heavenly Father for his protecting care and rich blessings in the first great voyage of life together. May His name ever be honored by our lives."

Thus began the voyage of life together for these two lives—open-eyed, imaginative, appreciative, interested in the great of all time and in the great out-of-doors of nature, and reverent toward God, who had made and now controlled it all.

A few weeks after their return from the honeymoon the Wingers settled at Indiana University, where Otho continued his college work while Ida enrolled in the department of art. After a year at the university he found it necessary to return to schoolteaching to earn more money to complete his university work. So he secured a position as principal of the high school at Sweetser, Indiana. He held this position for two years. It was here that their first son, Robert, was born on August 20, 1903.

In the summer of 1905, he again returned to the university to continue his studies. During that summer he received his Bachelor of Arts degree. In the fall he received an appointment as superintendent of schools at Hope, Indiana. However, he kept up his studies at Indiana University and returned to the university as soon as his school was out. The same arrangement continued for the school year 1906-1907. While they were living at Hope, the second son, Paul, was born on April 10, 1907. In the spring of 1907, Otho received his Master of Arts degree at Indiana University.

It is typical of Otho Winger that he completed two or three years of his college work and one year of graduate work while missing only one year of teaching. He worked summer and winter, probably day and night, to achieve his goal. After receiving his Master of Arts degree at Indiana University, he received a call to come to Manchester College to teach history and education. He accepted the call, moved his family to North Manchester, and began his work. This connection with Manchester College was to continue thirty-four years, during which time great changes took place in the college.

IDA MILLER WINGER

Ida Miller was the descendant of a long line of Dunker ancestors. Her paternal grandfather was Michael Miller, who had married Phoebe Bigler for a second wife. To this union were born fifteen children. On the maternal side, her grandfather was Marcus A. Cupp, who had married Elizabeth Brower in Allen County, Ohio. She was a member of a prominent Brethren family and this likely accounts for the fact that he changed his membership from the Lutheran to the Brethren Church. Both these grandfathers moved to western Missouri with their families for a time; there Amos, the son of the Millers, met and married Sarah, the daughter of the Cupps. Both the Miller and the Cupp family later moved to Wabash County, Indiana. To Amos and Sarah Miller was born on August 31, 1875, a daughter, Ida, who became the wife of Otho Winger.

Ida was born in a country home on the Wabash-Kosciusko county line, near North Manchester. The family soon moved to a home about two miles west of North Manchester. Here they lived for many years and here Ida grew up. The home was about a half mile from the West Manchester Church of the Brethren. By the church lot stood the Acme school, where she received her grade school education and later taught. Here on the school ground, when a girl of ten, she received an injury to her hip which gave her lifelong trouble and ultimately undermined her health, perhaps leading to her death.

Ida taught at the Acme school from 1895 to

1897 and then from 1897 to 1899 at the Fruitdale and Citronelle seminaries in Alabama. She entered Manchester College in 1899 but soon was asked to do some teaching in the commercial department. A little later she did full-time teaching and was so employed when she married in 1902.

Two girlhood friends of Mrs. Winger were Orpha Funk, later Mrs. A. R. Bridge, and Alice King. Mrs. Bridge and Mrs. Winger taught school in adjoining counties and continued a warm friendship throughout life. Alice King was a teacher at Manchester College for a time, then married Adam Ebey. She and her husband gave thirty years of able service to the India mission field. These women maintained a warm friendship throughout life.

Ida was a tall, attractive woman. She always stood erect and carried herself with dignity. She dressed neatly and was an efficient housekeeper and a rapid worker, with quick movements and an energetic walk.

Ida was two years older that Otho. She was teaching at Manchester when he was a student. They became "friends" in about 1901. This friendship grew into love, and their marriage followed. For many years separation was a painful experience for each of them. Her letters abound with expressions of loneliness and of affection for him. "We get along after a fashion but the joy is gone when you are away and it seems so empty." "It seems so long, so long since we have had you, dear, and little Paul laments so much that Papa is gone." And on Sunday morning, June 25, 1914, she wrote: "I have been with you in spirit today and now as you are

Otho Winger as a Boy

As a Very Young Preacher

Expostulating to a Friend

Otho and Ida; Wedding Picture

Ida Miller Winger

standing before your audience I am trying to help hold up your hands."

In 1913 Mrs. Winger was troubled with a throat affliction and had to be in Chicago for treatment for a few months, while Otho carried on at home with Robert and Paul, who were then ten and six respectively. Their letters, which were daily and often twice daily during this time, are filled with expressions of the most tender affection and devotion.

As the responsibilities of college and church increased and brought more separations, it was an object of regret to both of them. Otho was gone a great deal. Opportunity for enjoying each other and for spending time with their growing boys was being given up for work and ever more work. The responsibilities of the home fell heavily on Mrs. Winger. He was aware of it and expressed regret and blamed himself almost to the point of giving up his college presidency, he said. But little could be done in the present situation. It was the price to be paid for the task he had assumed.

Mrs. Winger was a good hostess, always willing to put on extra plates and feed unannounced visitors when her generous husband invited them to meals. Their home became for many years a veritable hotel where guests of the college found a warm welcome and were graciously received.

Mrs. Winger was never rugged in health. We have noted the difficulty with her throat in 1913. All through her life she had trouble on occasion with the hip she had injured in childhood. Yet she kept up the home, raised two boys, mostly by herself, helped her husband in the office when needed and managed to travel a great deal.

One finds it exceedingly difficult to see how Mrs. Winger did so much traveling. Often she complained of being tired in her hips or legs. She suffered from sciatica, lumbago, and other complications. And yet she would travel with her husband on fast, long, and rugged auto trips to the Grand Canyon, to New England, to Texas, to Florida—in fact, to every state in the Union and finally on a trip around the world.

Mr. Winger had boundless energy and rugged strength. They walked a great deal on their world trip. Again and again Mrs. Winger's diary records, "I was so tired I could go no more. We took a taxi back and then Otho went out again." Before they left Jerusalem she wrote, "We took a walk around the city walls. The walls are 2½ miles around, but we walked about five miles, but I was so tired I could hardly get back, laid down and did not get up for two hours, not even for lunch." In India she sometimes took what she called a dandy (a chair carried between two bamboo poles). In China and perhaps in Japan she was pulled at times in a jinrikisha. On her return on the boat she had a very severe attack of sciatica and had to be brought from California to Indiana in a Pullman sleeper.

Ida had been brought up in the Puritan tradition common to most Brethren homes of that day. The religious consciousness typical of Puritanism remained with her through life. As they approached Milan, Italy, on their journey she recorded this sentence in her diary: "The Lord has wonderfully blest and cared for us on our journey." The strict social ideals of Puritanism remained with her through life, especially as they relate to temperance and problems of social morality. To the last she was loathe to eat in a restaurant or hotel where any kind of intoxicating liquor was sold.

One of the impressive notes throughout Mrs. Winger's diary on her trip around the world was the comments she made about the condition of women. In many lands they do the hard, dirty work and live in almost impossible conditions. Upon leaving India she said:

One of the things that impressed me most was the condition of India's women, I mean of the largest class. They are so ignorant, can't read or write, their homes are such dirty, dark, unpleasant places. They must do the hardest work, carry such immense loads on their heads, have so little for clothing, so little for anything, work on the floor, eat on the floor, sit on the floor, and many sleep on the floor, have nothing artistic or beautiful, have no ambitions, must cling to their caste, and can never rise out of it and by the men are looked upon as nothing. The dirtiest, most menial work must be done by their hands. What can we do for them?

Mrs. Winger loved cleanliness. She abhorred dirty houses and dirty faces, of which she saw many on her travels. Her diaries abound with references to clean restaurants, clean hotel rooms, clean homes, clean-faced people, and very often also to dirty places and dirty faces. On occasion she would say of some group that they were the dirtiest she had yet seen. Her love of cleanliness and neatness also led her to protest frequently against her husband's lack of concern about the "niceties" of dress.

She also had a keen sense of beauty which found expression in her love of good pictures. She had studied art at Indiana University and did some painting. She was alerted to beauty of line and color. In her diaries are found descriptions of beauty as she saw it in pictures, in buildings, in the landscape, or in other nature scenes. One such entry says, "Thru the Swiss Alps the buildings are very pretty. Some artistic touches to all, small cultivated patches, terraced mountain sides. As we wound along through these valleys there were always mountains on either hand with their green trees, homes, villages, snow-capped, craggy mountains, deep ravines. It was one long picture of beauty."

As they left Smyrna by boat, she wrote:

I watched the sunset. The first sunset I had seen at sea and it was the most beautiful, the most gorgeous splendor I ever saw. Words are too small to describe the golden glow on the clouds, the flame of the sun as it sank behind the clouds, and over to one side the most beautiful rose and gray combinations my eyes have ever beheld. The golden glow in the mountain, too, was most beautiful.

Mrs. Winger had a skilled hand. She was a teacher of shorthand and could help out at the office in emergencies or on holidays when regular workers were gone. She was an excellent seamstress, and kept a live interest in rare patterns. She loved laces and kept up working in them and purchasing beautiful new designs.

In the Winger household, college students found a home and an opportunity to help pay their way through college. Mary Shaeffer, Nettie Senger, and Geneva George are but a few of those who lived in the home and thus found college a possibility.

Throughout a lifetime as wife, mother, and fellow traveler, Mrs. Winger also kept alive an interest in the local church and Sunday school, in the women's work of the church, in missionary study groups, and in the College Woman's Club. As her husband kept alive an active interest in all the movements of college and church, so she also was interested.

After President Winger's illness and retirement they lived at the west end of North Manchester, approximately two miles from the college. Mrs. Winger missed the college activities and her close association with college friends. She and her sister Edith kept the large home and took good care of Otho. Mrs. Winger was much concerned with his increased affliction, while the trouble in her hip grew more serious year by year. By late 1943 her case became serious. Her last months on earth were months of suffering. Her hip gave her much trouble and her suffering was intense. Other complications set in. She went to the Bluffton Hospital, was returned for a while, but went to the hospital again; there she died on January 29, 1944.

These words may not portray the story of her life adequately but those who lived in the community with her will remember her as a woman of efficiency, of personal dignity, and of deep concern about things that matter. There can be no doubt that in this case, as in many others, the strength of the man out front fighting public battles for church and college was in no small degree dependent for strength and inspiration on the good woman back home who gave him all her love and devotion.

Otho Winger as a Teacher

Otho Winger returned to Manchester College as a teacher in 1907 while E. M. Crouch was president. L. D. Ikenberry was then treasurer of the college, and I. B. Book held the title of secretary. The college was only twelve years old as a Brethren institution. There was at that time not a very strong interest in higher education in the Church of the Brethren. The college was tolerated but not taken into the affections and confidence of the church people generally. Moreover, Mount Morris College, at Mount Morris, Illinois, was older and stronger, and was attracting many students from Indiana and Ohio and elsewhere. As a result Manchester was poorly attended, and the financial condition of the college was precarious indeed. The professors were paid unbelievably meager salaries. Each fall there was anxiety as to whether there would be enough students to operate.

When Otho Winger returned to Manchester he was thirty years old, strong, vigorous, and energetic. He located in a little frame house on Wayne Street a few blocks from the college. Here he began his prodigious work: gardening, teaching, lecturing, and preaching on Sunday. The writer remembers seeing him during this time on a Sunday morning driving out to a near-by church with his father-in-law's mule hitched to an open carriage. The mule may have been unusual, but going in the carriage was surely not.

Otho Winger was called to the college to teach history and education, but the first term he was here he taught also English, Latin, and philosophy. Later he taught in still other fields, such as Greek, geography, and Bible. He used to say in his characteristically jovial way that he had taught almost everything in the curriculum except music. Once he made a mistake in sending a list of teachers to be approved by the trustees and got his own name into the list of teachers for the music department. One of the trustees with a sense of humor replied, "I admire your pluck, but I am afraid you will not succeed as a music teacher. Which department did you mean? I will be satisfied with you in almost any department except music!" He often referred to this with a hearty laugh.

In the writer's days as a student, from 1908 to 1913, Otho Winger was teaching chiefly English, history, and philosophy. After the college grew and his duties of administration increased, he taught chiefly philosophy, especially a full year's course to seniors. It was not the writer's privilege to take the course in philosophy, but of the other subjects taught it seemed to him that Professor Winger did equally well in literature and in history. His contagious enthusiasm made historical or literary characters live and this made learning easy.

When Professor Winger began his teaching he taught as many as thirty classes a week. He had unusual stores of energy and worked long hours, yet in his *Memories of Manchester* he declared these to have been the easiest years of his life.

Otho Winger was a great teacher. He would have been so regarded in any college or university. The author has studied at the University of Chicago and Columbia University and has come into contact with many great teachers; and yet Otho Winger still stands out as one of the two or three very greatest teachers he has ever had. Naturally, because he taught over wide areas of knowledge his mastery of detail or his depth of scholarship in any field could not be extremely thorough, but his breadth of knowledge in many fields and his enthusiasm and pulsating energy compensated for this lack.

There were at least five qualities that made of him a great teacher. They were his forceful personality, his enthusiasm, his clear knowledge, his marvelous memory, and his love of people. Otho Winger was a personality to be reckoned with in any group. He was large, broad shouldered, with a heavy torso, a genial, kindly face, topped by a heavy shock of hair, and small, attractive hands. His mental processes were rapid; his voice was strong and carried well. The force of his personality made a strong impression on students and naturally made his teaching more effective.

He had remarkable enthusiasm. He went to his classes with enthusiasm and had power to transmit this enthusiasm to his students. He came to his office and pitched into his work with a vigor that made difficult tasks yield to his energy. His chapel announcements often gathered momentum and created enthusiasm among students and faculty. A faculty member with drooping spirits needed but to step into his office for a while and either watch him work or listen to some story or to some plan for the college, and then he could go back to his task with renewed spirit.

He had a keen mind that had a clear grasp on vast stores of knowledge. His mental processes were more rapid than those of most men among whom he worked. He seemed intuitively to reach correct answers to problems which other men reached only by labored reasoning. He had insight into human character and a clear grasp of philosophic truth. He was not a teacher who was inclined to balance fine-spun theories one against the other and leave the conclusion dangle in thin air. He reached conclusions and announced a philosophy of life which was always constructive, positive, hopeful, and wholesome. There was nothing anemic or weak about him. His influence on students was exhilarating.

Otho Winger had a remarkable memory. It seems in part a family trait. Other members of the family too had prodigious memories. He could remember obscure dates and remote places in history; he could quote many long poems from end to end. He could give the names of all the kings and princes of Europe, and seemingly knew everyone's lineage to remote ancestors. His history students had to be able to write out family genealogies of the leading royal families of Europe. A group of us guessed one day what the questions in an examination in European history would be. We all expected we would have to name the kings of England, France, or Germany. Sure enough, we had guessed correctly. His students needed to be able to draw maps showing the military campaigns of the Civil War, indicating rivers, creeks, battlefields, the movements of troops, and the generals in charge. Students in literature were expected to know the lives of the authors in detail and the identity of poems and books, and to be able to quote freely from the poems.

This may seem dry learning. But he made a sort of game out of it, and it was most interesting. The force of his personality and the enthusiasm with which he did his work made it fascinating. Then, too, Otho Winger loved people. It made no difference whether the person involved was prepossessing in appearance or had social standing. It often seemed that the less one was accepted by society generally the more Professor Winger would be interested in him. His interest was not limited to the young. He liked old and young folks alike. Little children felt the kindliness and geniality of his personality; old people, especially if suffering, felt the tenderness and sympathy in his make-up. Young people felt the strength, the vigor, and the enthusiasm of his personality. All of them liked him because he seemed to have a genuine love and concern for them. No one seeing him among students, in a church audience, or in a group of men could doubt his natural outgoing love of people.

These qualities—force of personality, enthusiasm, breadth of knowledge, a strong memory, love of people—made him a great teacher.

One of his students from the Hope high school days, writing about him, says:

OTHO WINGER AS A TEACHER

I can see him vividly as he appeared in the Hope days . . . a rather large man, broad of face, broad of shoulder, black hair, smooth shaven and dressed in his Dunker black coat, a dark man with a rather pale German face. I can almost hear his voice, but not honestly enough to describe. I can recall some of his gestures, one a habit of standing somewhat "a-slant," with his fine white hands in restrained gesture.

In Channing's *Students History of the United States,* which I bought in January, 1907, I find this in my round girlhood hand: "No president has ever done a more unconstitutional act, I should say no president has ever done a greater act unless it was Abraham Lincoln than Thomas Jefferson when he bought the Louisiana Territory.—Professor Winger."

In a letter to President Winger, Andrew W. Cordier, one of his most capable students, once wrote:

When I came to Manchester College I had the pleasure of having you as one of my teachers in Medieval History. When I went to the University some one of our Dunker friends was belittling the intellectual strength of our small colleges. I remember of telling him that I never had anyone in the University who had given me more material and had given it so convincingly and in such a well-organized fashion as had President Winger of Manchester College.

In order to see this teacher through the eyes of others who studied under him, letters of inquiry were sent out to a number of his former students; several of their replies or excerpts from them are here included:

During the school year of 1907-08 I took the first of many courses under President Winger. It was Ancient, Mediaeval and Modern History. The class met on the second floor of Bumgerdner Hall. We often gathered

43

about him after dismissal to listen to what seemed to us an overflow from an inexhaustible store of knowledge about the characters whom he had brought to life for us. One scene stands out vividly in my mind: We had followed him down the stairway through the hall and out onto the walk which led from Bumgerdner to the Chapel; he all the while discoursing upon the subject for which the class hour was only sufficient to get him started and to stimulate our interest. The class session did not cease until we had taken our places in Chapel! — *R. H. Miller, professor of religion and philosophy, Manchester College.*

President Winger was my teacher in Bible History in the year 1913-14. This was my first year in college. I will list some of the impressions that remain as I look back on that experience. Probably no course in my college experience has given me more satisfaction than has the Bible History under President Winger. It helped me organize my Biblical knowledge, particularly from a chronological standpoint and this has been invaluable to me as a Sunday School teacher throughout the years.

I remember him as a vigorous and brusque teacher. He literally filled the room and dominated the situation. There was no question who was in charge of the class. But along with his aggressiveness, there was a kindly sympathetic touch that made me feel he had a very personal interest in me. He was frank and straight forward. He did not hestitate to condemn sin and wrong wherever it was found.

His honesty and sincerity made a deep impression on me. As I look back over the years, I consider him as one of the men who had a vital part in the shaping of my life and for this I am deeply indebted to him.—*Carl W. Holl, former dean of Manchester College.*

As a teacher, Dr. Winger immediately gave the impression that he possessed a great fund of information about the subject, was not bound by a textbook, but somehow had a great grasp of the field in which he was teaching. His anecdotes and illustrations highlighted the recitations. It was always a pleasure to enter his class for the unexpected was sure to happen. No student was ever put on the spot, yet each one felt it his duty to know his lesson. — *Norman B. Wine, assistant superintendent of schools, Dayton, Ohio.*

I shall have to agree with you on one point; that is, he was a great teacher. In fact he had the quality of a great man in other lines of endeavor than that of teaching. For, he was a superior type of individual in many respects.

The presence of his great personality filled the classroom and was felt by every student. He led and directed the thinking of his students, challenging each and every one to do his or her best. He was thorough himself and expected the same from those whom he endeavored to teach. He was possessed with a good sense of humor and a hearty laugh. Hence, there was never a dull moment in his classes. He took a personal interest in each one of his students. He was easy of approach, making it possible for one to discuss with him, if he cared to do so, his individual problems.

I count myself fortunate to have had this great man, Otho Winger, as a teacher and friend.—*I. J. Sollenberger, School of Business Administration, Department of Finance, University of Oklahoma.*

I shall always be grateful to God for the touch of Otho Winger on my life. He taught me that "truth is *always* from God." One of his words often used was "magnanimous" and he roused the desire to achieve magnanimity in oneself. We wanted to be like him. He profoundly impressed me by his robust Biblical faith and when combined with his idea of all truth as being from God, its effect has been most pervading. Few days of my teaching life when I don't think of Winger.

He exemplified in his own person that greatness and nobility are based upon simplicity and unselfishness.— *F. E. Mallott, professor of church history, Bethany Biblical Seminary, Chicago.*

There are four definite things which come to my mind very quickly when I think of Otho as a great teacher. They are as follows:

1. His love for and interest in his students. This was evident both in and out of the classroom. Even when he disciplined a student this point was evident to the one being disciplined.
2. His enthusiastic interest in the subject being taught. This is rather closely related to the third point.
3. His ability to arouse the interest of his students in the subject being taught. This always comes to my mind when I think of him as a teacher. When I enrolled for the first time in one of his history classes I did so with the feeling that here is just one of those dry, uninteresting subjects that is required of me. I had no intention of doing more than get a credit in the subject. Before the course was finished I was thinking of the possibility of making history my major subject. That is just what I did. History and geography have been my major interest from that time to this day. In fact my interest in maps, which has been responsible for the major portion of my life's work really dates from the history courses taken with Otho Winger.
4. His friendly personality which brought the love and respect of all those who came in contact with him was certainly one of the large factors which made him one of the greatest teachers of his day.—*D. E. Sites, representative of Rand McNally & Company.*

A loving tribute to a great man. President Winger taught history with such vivacious energy that it seemed he had experienced it. The people of by-gone ages were as real to him as present-day associates. His ardor was contagious and made one wish to know the past as he knew it. But to me his most outstanding characteristic was his concern for the church and his willingness to serve with all his dynamic personality. He was first of all a great churchman."—*Mary Stoner Wine, wife of Pastor G. L. Wine.*

Otho Winger as a Teacher

Otho Winger was, in my judgment, a truly outstanding teacher. His primary interest was in the student. He had a great mind and a warm heart. I would say that he was utterly human and all of his students felt him to be a personal friend. When I was a student in Manchester College, the school was very small so that we were quite close to the teachers. Otho Winger impressed us by his genuine devotion to his students. He had an unbounded enthusiasm and a physical vitality that was stimulating. His capacity to remember facts was always a source of admiration. He loved to teach and this natural and enthusiastic spirit made it rather easy for his pupils to follow and to learn. President Winger has left an abiding influence not only upon Manchester College but upon all the students who knew him. He was a man of great faith and believed in the college without reservation. A lesser spirit would have given up in despair many a time. In my judgment even the apparent weaknesses were indications of his strength. Sometimes we felt he undertook too much but it was his amazing vitality which had to find expression in many ways. No one will ever be able to think of Manchester College without thinking of Otho Winger. For many years he was in reality the College. He was my friend whom I remember with deep gratitude. —*H. A. Studebaker, pastor, Congregational church, Lake Worth, Florida.*

President Otho Winger was outstanding as a preacher, teacher, churchman, author, traveller, administrator and friend. No other man besides my father influenced my life and work so much as he. It was a privilege to have been his neighbor and coworker.—*Lawrence W. Shultz, professor, Manchester College.*

Otho Winger was a great teacher. He was a great teacher because he was a great character and lost himself in giving inspiration and direction to the learning and thinking of others. He was interested in his students, both for what they were, and for what they might become.

He had a great mind and kept himself mentally alert

by prodigious reading and thinking. He respected and had confidence in his students, and obtained his highest satisfaction in stimulating, and in observing the development of all in his classes.

One could agree with him without his becoming proud and one could disagree with him without his becoming offended. In his teaching he was the embodiment of the doctrine of the "second mile."—*Dr. W. W. Peters, alumnus of 1915, formerly president of McPherson College.*

I was a Freshman student in Professor Winger's class in English in Manchester College 1910-11, the year before he was elected to the presidency of the College. In my estimation, these were some of the major things that made Otho Winger a great teacher: He had a wealth of creative imagination which he controlled and turned into productive channels. He read widely and critically in the field, and illustrated his lectures and comments pointedly from his reading as well as from his personal experiences and observations. He made thorough preparation for his class sessions. He was tolerant of conflicting points of view that did not violate what he regarded as fundamental principles. Coupled with that, he was broad in sympathies. He was a good practical psychologist. And above all, he was deeply and sincerely interested in each of his students and in their ultimate welfare, putting their interests ahead of his own, giving of his time unstintingly to them, being a friend to each one of them, offering encouragement and warning wherever and whenever he saw the need.

As one example: During one class session he evidently came to the conclusion that my twenty-year old idealism needed tempering by some degree of realism. So for the next hour after class he talked with me on the subject, although there were important things that he had intended to do during that hour.—*W. Arthur Cable, head of the Department of Speech, University of Arizona.*

Dr. Winger was a master of the arts of teaching. But beyond this, he had that quality of heart — that all

Otho Winger at Forty

A Characteristic Chapel Pose

pervading interest in the lives of his students—that is the quality most esteemed in those we remember as our great teachers.—*Paul Mort, professor, Columbia University.*

If we were to base our estimate of him as measured by modern methods I do not think he would rate so high, but if we consider that inspiration to the love of learning is the mark of a good teacher, I think he was in a class by himself. He did some remarkable things along that line.

He took a group of country boys and girls, some poorly prepared for college and by his personality and enthusiasm moulded them into a group of students in the real sense of the word. I remember one class of students in American History was required to memorize long lists of dates, events and places. Some objected because memorization was in dispute, but that has been to my advantage in my own teaching and public work. — *A. M. Stout, alumnus of 1912.*

While in attendance at Manchester College it was my good fortune to have Otho Winger as one of my teachers. I considered him one of the four best teachers I have known as nearly as I am able to evaluate them. He was most industrious in his work; he gave me the impression that he was consecrating his efforts to his work; I considered him highly capable; he had the enthusiasm and the zest of a great teacher; as I remember him he was always well prepared for each class period; while [he was] quite human in his contacts with his pupils in class we had no doubt . . . that he expected us to do the best we could do each day; neither was there any doubt about Dr. Winger working as hard or harder than any of his students.— *R. D. Shaffer, superintendent of schools, Muncie, Indiana.*

One course given by President Winger after his administrative duties made it impossible to teach more than one class was a year's work in philosophy, already mentioned. Many of the best seniors took this course. The writer was dean of the college for a decade of this time. It was the testimony of scores of students that this was the best or one of the very best courses in college. Here in the classroom his mind was entirely free and he examined every question with a completely open mind. His mastery in this field was marvelous in light of the fact that he was overwhelmed with a host of administrative detail. Here he was a scholar, with complete academic freedom, willing to examine every philosophic question without bias.

President Winger would have been considered a top-flight teacher in any college or university in which he might have chosen to work.

Otho Winger as the Builder of a College

The history of Manchester College to date is inextricably interwoven with the name and career of Otho Winger. He entered Manchester nine years after the college had its beginnings under the United Brethren Church and three years after it was purchased by the Church of the Brethren. He went out to raise money to save it from bankruptcy while he was yet a student in 1901. He returned to teach in Manchester College in 1907, became vice-president of the college in 1910, and president in 1911. This latter post he held for thirty years, during which the college grew from a weak, struggling, non-standard, preparatory, Bible, and commercial school to a fully standardized liberal arts college, annually enrolling more than one thousand students.

What is now Manchester College was founded by the United Brethren Church at Roanoke, Indiana. In 1889 it was moved to North Manchester, Indiana. D. N. Howe, its first president, literally hewed a place for it out of the forest on the northeast edge of the town and began operations in the fall of 1889. For five years he struggled heroically to keep it alive and growing. During 1894-1895 another president, a Mr. Kriebel, was at the helm. Simultaneously, the Brethren under the leadership of L. T.

Holsinger, E. S. Young, S. S. Young, David Hollinger, L. H. Eby, and others were preparing to estab-
lish a college; in 1895 they purchased the institution
from the United Brethren and began schoolwork
in that year, with E. S. Young as president and S. S.
Young as secretary. (Incidentally, there was never
any relation between the United Brethren Church
and the Church of the Brethren. They had entirely
different origins and never had any organic relationship.)

The purpose of the school was "to promote the
interest of education in general and especially
among the children of the German Baptist Brethren." (The name of the church was changed in
1908 from *German Baptist Brethren Church* to the
Church of the Brethren.) The object of the Bible
school was to promote Biblical instruction particularly on the denominational line of the German
Baptist Church. All trustees were to be members
of the church. They operated the college in the
name of the church and took full responsibility for
financing the school, many of the trustees sacrificing
heroically to keep it alive.

One of the truths which our generation has
learned but which was not so well understood fifty
years ago is that a college is not self-supporting.
While the church gave some money to the mainte-
nance of the college during the period from 1895
to 1902, it was not enough to keep the school from
running hopelessly into debt.

This became evident in 1901. It was then that
Elder I. D. Parker from Goshen, Indiana, offered
to turn his share of the college over to the church

if the church would take it, and he was sure the other trustees would do the same. He then went to various district meetings of the church and asked if they would take over the college if it were turned over free of debt. The Northwestern Ohio, Southern Illinois, Northern Indiana, Middle Indiana, and Southern Ohio districts of the Church of the Brethren agreed to do this.

I. D. Parker, assisted by Otho Winger and others, then went out and raised twenty-seven thousand dollars to free the college from debt, and on May 6, 1902, the college was turned over to trustees who had been elected by the church. They then entered into articles of agreement to operate the college "in the interest of Christian education under the auspices of the German Baptist Brethren Church." They agreed that no debt should ever be put on the real estate or personal property of the college.

The trustees, however, did not operate the college themselves, but leased it to a group of men who operated it. It seems that the buildings and equipment were put at the disposal of these brethren, who then took the risk of operating the college and accepting whatever profit or loss resulted from the enterprise. This period of lease extended from 1902 to 1910, during which time E. M. Crouch was president, L. D. Ikenberry was treasurer, I. B. Book was secretary, and, at intervals, T. S. Moherman and M. M. Sherrick shared in the lease.

These men found it hard going, and at times had very little income to show for their efforts. Educational sentiment was but slight in the church and financial support was meager. Year after year they labored on, hoping that the next year would be better. Students were few, financial conditions were stringent, and the outlook was discouraging. Teachers taught for salaries that make present-day teachers gasp for breath.

The writer of these pages was a student at Manchester College in the spring terms of 1904 and 1906, during the summers of 1908, 1909, and 1910, and during the entire school year of 1909-1910. The college plant in 1904 consisted of three small buildings. The library was housed in a small room in the Bible school building and could not have consisted of more than a few thousand volumes. There was no organized athletic program and so, of course, no intercollegiate athletic contests.

I well remember that when college opened in the fall of 1909 I, with some other students and Dr. P. B. Fitzwater, the Bible teacher of that day, stood on the campus talking about enrollment possibilities. I think only about sixty-five students had yet enrolled, whereupon Dr. Fitzwater expressed a concern as to whether we would have enough students to justify operating the college that year.

Despite these conditions some progress was made during this era. Although there were achievements, the income was insufficient to continue the plan of leasing the school. It was apparent that the method of leasing the college was not satisfactory. The church itself felt too little responsibility for the school. The lessees were carrying the load too largely by themselves. It had become apparent that something that would serve as a "shot in the arm"

needed to be done if the institution was to survive.
So, on June 1, 1910, the college was turned over to
the trustees, who were to assume the general management and control of the school. The new plan
was presented to the church districts and, while
some hesitated, a plan was devised by which teachers' contracts should become void if they were not
paid within thirty days after becoming due. This
plan is said to have been presented by Otho Winger.
With this plan the trustees took control of the institution. In after years President Winger often
referred to this ingenious idea by which the college
could operate without fear of debt.

The trustees elected the officers and employed
the teachers. In their name all the money was
raised and the property was held. Since trustees
were not educators and were scattered afar they
elected an executive committee which was to operate the college in harmony with the general policies
outlined by the trustees. It was at this point, in
1910, that Otho Winger as vice-president became
an active agent for the promotion of the college.

Some alumni and others felt that the new president should have a Doctor of Philosophy degree.
Dr. M. G. Brumbaugh, veteran Brethren educator,
was consulted; he recommended Dr. E. C. Bixler,
who had just taken his doctor's degree at the University of Pennsylvania. So we find in the minutes
of the board of trustees for January 1910 this item:
"By ballot the following Executive Board was elected: President, E. C. Bixler; Vice-president, Otho
Winger; Secretary, L. D. Ikenberry." This executive board was then authorized to arrange a faculty

for the school year 1910-1911. The trustees present at this meeting were Frank Fisher, Jacob Coppock, J. D. Mishler, and Manly Deeter; the secretary of the board, L. W. Teeter, was absent.

Dr. Bixler was then thirty-three years of age, unmarried. He was a classical scholar, having given much of his time to a study of the ancient languages. He came to Manchester when it had relatively little of the literary interest and the cultural atmosphere of well-established Eastern colleges. He was married in December of the first year of his presidency and he and his bride were housed in the boys' dormitory. Though the records do not give reasons, this arrangement did not continue. In his *Memories of Manchester* President Winger says: "By the close of the year both he and the trustees felt they wanted to make another change."

We find in the records of the board of trustees this minute from their meeting on January 10, 1911: "After a discussion of the members of the present Executive Board of the faculty with view to its reorganization, Brother Otho Winger was by ballot elected its President, and Brother L. D. Ikenberry its Secretary-Treasurer." The trustees present for this election were Frank Fisher, D. B. Garber, Jacob Coppock, Manly Deeter, and G. A. Snyder; L. W. Teeter was absent because of illness.

This simple minute records a most significant event in the life of Manchester College. Otho Winger had no Doctor of Philosophy degree. In his *Memories of Manchester* he said:

I was not ambitious for any such job. I came to Manchester hoping to get a few years of college teaching

56

and get a little money so I could go on to the University and take my doctor's degree, and teach history in some college and spend some time in writing books.

I shall never forget the night the trustees called me in and said that I had been elected President of the College. I frankly told them that I didn't think they had selected me because I was best fitted for the presidency, but because they thought I was about as well-fitted to break my neck trying as anyone else they knew.

I knew the situation and outlook for the school were not good, but I did not know it all. Could I have seen what I would have to go through I would certainly have refused; and yet after thirty years, seeing the development and progress of the institution, I am glad to have had something to do with it in one of its most trying periods.

During the last two years before President Winger took over the presidency of the college the outlook was indeed not encouraging. Up to this time Manchester was really not much of a college in the modern sense. Very few students who came to Manchester were of collegiate standing. Most of them were listed as preparatory, Normal English (a teachers' preparatory course), commerce, elocution, or Bible students. Only a very few ranked as college students. In 1898-1899 the college had five liberal arts, eighty-three preparatory, thirty-one business, thirteen shorthand and typewriting, forty-seven music, and twenty-four Bible students. In fact, Manchester College graduated only two students from the collegiate department in 1900, none in 1901, one in 1902, one in 1903, none in 1904, one in 1910, none in 1911, three each in 1912 and 1913, and eight in 1914. From that time on, college graduating classes grew rapidly.

OTHO WINGER AS THE BUILDER OF A COLLEGE

At the outset of the Winger administration there were four buildings on the campus: Bumgerdner Hall, the first building, erected in 1889; the Bible school building, erected in 1896; a ladies' dormitory, built in 1898; and a men's dormitory, built in 1906. All of these were relatively small buildings, quite economically constructed. They were useful but certainly were not elaborate or substantially built.

The faculty was small and had limited training. In all, twenty-five names are listed for 1911-1912, many of them assistant and part-time teachers. None of the teachers held a Doctor of Philosophy degree; only four had a Master of Arts degree; six held a Bachelor of Arts degree. The other fifteen held various minor degrees or none. The total annual enrollment for the year 1908-1909 had been three hundred twenty; for the year 1909-1910 it was two hundred one; for the following year it was two hundred two. This meant that the enrollment at any one time was probably as low as one hundred fifty or one hundred sixty.

The year before Otho Winger became the president of the college it had experienced a deficit of several thousand dollars. And, in addition, educational sentiment in the church owning the college was very low. It was not popular in many churches to be an open advocate of college education. Even the town of North Manchester seemed to doubt whether this struggling institution had any future and apparently looked askance at this new president who had the notion that he could build a college.

The writer has never known anyone who so

completely identified himself and his lifework with the job to which he was called as did Otho Winger. He often told the story of the boy who had a dog and told his friends, "If you want to like me you've got to like my dog." So if you wanted to like Otho Winger you had to like his college. He was for anything or anyone who in a legitimate way could further the interests of Manchester College. He was ready to work for it literally day and night and to do battle for it against its detractors. I recall that when a disgruntled alumnus was spreading reports of the unorthodoxy of the Bible teaching at Manchester, Otho Winger got in his car and drove to a neighboring state to face the accuser and challenge his reports. The welfare of Manchester was his meat and drink. For many years he impressed his co-workers with a complete, unreserved identification of himself with the college. His complete self-abandonment to its welfare was the marvel of his friends. Indeed, he seemed to many as the personification of the college, and the growth of the college seemed like the unfoldment of his purpose.

It soon became evident that the trustees of the college had been wise in the selection of a president. In the first place, Otho Winger had an intelligent view of what it would take to build a college to fit the needs of his constituency. Second, he both had and was willing to devote his marvelous energy to accomplish the task. Third, he had the ability to win friends; and, fourth, he had an uncanny way of bringing things to pass.

The story of his work in building the college has been told quite freely by him in his *Memories of Manchester.* It would be like carrying coals to Newcastle to repeat the story in detail. But building the college was so large a part of his life that it cannot be omitted. The writer, who was on the faculty for the first sixteen years of the Winger presidency and was in close touch with it during the other fourteen, can only review some of the more significant developments, indicate the role played by President Winger, and point out some of his unique qualities as a college president.

Soon after he was elected to head the institution things began to happen. The student enrollment increased. The faculty was enlarged; buildings were built or old ones enlarged; the constituency of the college was extended so that instead of each year seeing a static institution fighting with its back to the wall, every year marked progress. Instead of waiting to see if there would be enough students to hold college, he and his associates went out after students, and brought them in.

MAKING FRIENDS

In a very revealing letter to an intimate friend, President Winger stated his point of view regarding the needs of the college at this time. In effect, it was this: The college had been largely without friends. It needed friends. We must do everything we can to make friends for it. "We must be friends to all. We must get close to them. . . . that's one of the things that counts. . . . I could have avoided many an inconvenience in my work but it is those acts for others that make friends, and it is friends for Manchester College that is making the work go."

In keeping with this philosophy he set out to make friends. He visited people in their homes. He entertained people in his home, both for meals and often for the night. When they came to the college he gave them a personally conducted tour over the campus and through the buildings, all the while telling enthusiastically about his dreams for the college. Those who worked with him in those days can remember seeing him talking, jesting, gesturing as he went with guests from building to building.

When he began his work as president there were not a few in the church who were still opposed to colleges. This was true of a number of the older elders who felt that the college would lead young people away from the simple life—especially in dress—and might encourage pride and worldliness. In one of the Ohio districts there was an influential older elder who was known to be opposed to much the college stood for. President Winger cultivated the man's friendship for some time and then persuaded him to visit the college. When he arrived President Winger laid aside all his work and took the elder all over the college and explained everything—even selling him the gymnasium idea. Finally he presented the elder in chapel in glowing terms and had him speak to students and faculty. It would be difficult for such a one to continue in opposition to the college. In fact, he soon afterward made a gift to it.

FACULTY

The faculty, as has been noted, was not very strong when President Winger took over. But since most of the students up to this time were of subcollegiate standing, studying in various other departments, it did not seem quite so necessary to have men of advanced training. There was very little money with which to employ the faculty; so he set about building a faculty.

As reported in his *Memories of Manchester,* he went to some former students who were teaching high school, suggesting that they return to college and teach classes in the academy, thus earning their expenses while continuing their studies in college. The writer was one of these and remembers President Winger's call at the Wakarusa (Indiana) high school, where he was then teaching, in the spring of 1911, and the president's talk to the high school history class. Mother Schwalm was more eager for her son to continue teaching high school at home and gave the president to understand that he was not very welcome. But the son went to Manchester then, and continued on the faculty until 1927, and returned to it again in 1941.

Other alumni who were thus brought to the faculty were Edward Kintner, Herbert A. Studebaker, L. W. Shultz, and W. W. Peters. Not only did President Winger make it possible for these men to finish college but he also assisted them with their graduate training by making allowances of from twenty-five to seventy-five dollars per month for them while doing so. All of these except H. A.

Studebaker returned to the college for some years of service afterwards. The service these men gave to the college is evidence of the soundness of the policy for that time.

As has been the policy in many small church colleges, President Winger drew heavily upon the alumni to build his faculty. At the close of his presidency fully two thirds of them were graduates of the college, and this was characteristic of his entire administration.

Some of these alumni were brought to the faculty early before they had much graduate training and were then encouraged to continue their studies in graduate schools. Not a few of them went forward and later secured their doctor's degrees. He had the ability to make young, inexperienced people believe that they could do difficult tasks—tasks beyond their ability and training—and usually they did them.

At the time of the First World War, President Winger asked the writer to teach a class of strong students a course in English poetry. Since history was his (the writer's) major, he demurred. President Winger insisted that he could handle the English; so he attempted it and for him—and I think also for the students — it was an enjoyable and profitable experience.

In fact, it was characteristic of President Winger to meet an emergency by getting people to attempt things they did not believe they could do.

It is the impression of the writer that President Winger did not spend much time searching for teacher prospects. It is not easy to determine how he found teachers. In his files were a number of recommendations from teachers' agencies; some of his teachers he selected from other colleges, people whom he had known. In a few cases he secured them directly from some university—excepting of course, those who were from his own alumni group.

The fact that he discovered and brought to the campus some very strong men of independent spirit would indicate that he really was willing to have that kind of faculty personnel. But he spent too little time actually seeking out that kind of person. It is the case with many college presidents that availability often determines who gets the job, and sometimes mediocrity finds its way into a faculty. Of course, salary considerations and conditions of service may also have made it necessary sometimes to accept men and women of lesser ability.

President Winger showed great skill in inspiring his teachers after he had secured them. His enthusiasm for the college, his faith in them, his expressions of confidence in their ability, and his own tremendous application to his task, stimulated his teachers to heroic efforts for the college.

If a teacher went to the president's office in the morning, he likely found that he had already been at work at his desk before and after breakfast. He would probably get up, walk back and forth in the office, give some interesting news or tell a story, and then, after running his hands through his hair and rubbing his hands together, pitch into his work again with enthusiasm and energy. The teacher probably returned to his office or classroom renewed in spirit and attacked his own job with great enthusiasm.

His ability to inspire was phenomenal. It was sincere and genuine. Often he sent a written word of appreciation on which a teacher could live for weeks. The following is an example:

I want to repeat what I have often told you that I have been very happy for your ability in your field, and for the wide-spread recognition you have received. You stand alone in your field, so far as our church is concerned and with the same recognition in our state and many others. . . . I shall be happy for whatever opportunities and recognition you may have in the future, and I believe they will come.

To another who had been offered a high place in another institution and had decided to remain at Manchester, he sent a letter containing the following:

First, I want to thank you for your decision to remain with Manchester College. I have never had for one moment any other desire or hope than this. At the same time, I would not stand in the way of any man accepting . . . a place that will mean the largest opportunity for service and development. But now that you have decided, I want to express my sincere thanks and deep appreciation of your interest in Manchester.

Personally, I believe you have decided right. For scholarship, for character and spiritual life, for loyalty to the college and the church back of it, you have become well known both among students and patrons. Your work is highly spoken of among our churches, wherever I go. Your work and influence in the school is such that all students must respect and confess its wholesome effects.

As for the future, it shall be my pleasure and effort to encourage in any way I can the largest field of service possible for you. I have come to place the highest estimate upon ability plus character and I am glad to encourage young men and women and older ones too to receive the benefit and blessings of such influence. I shall be pleased to help in any way I can to increase your influence and service both in the school and in the church. I have great respect and confidence in your judgment on educational and other problems connected with our work. . . . I thank you for all the kind consideration you have given me in this work together and I want to show to you the same consideration. . . . I am anxious for Manchester to continue and to grow as a dynamic power for righteousness and for the Kingdom. To this end we need the ablest and best men and women working together here to accomplish the highest possible accomplishment for a Christian College to train men and women for loyal and efficient service in the Kingdom of God.

One of the ablest of his teachers wrote to Otho Winger: "Your appreciation of my work has been one of the most stimulating factors in my life's work."

Another writes of him: "I am deeply grateful for many favors shown me by President Winger. My debt to him can never be fully paid."

And still another writes: "As I have told you before you have been a source of inspiration to me for more than twenty years. I shall always attribute what little success I have achieved to your encouragement and help and for that reason I shall never cease to be grateful to you."

The man who was on President Winger's faculty as a teacher throughout the whole of his administration writes this general letter of appreciation of the work of President Winger. It was written by Professor Edward Kintner in 1941.

Dear President Winger:

Because of my "temporary retirement," when others were writing you last spring I did not get to do my share; so I want to take the opportunity afforded by your birthday to write a bit in appreciation of your service and to offer my congratulations on your sixty-fourth milestone. I sincerely hope that with greatly increased health you will have many more birthdays.

Then I want to add my contribution to that of the many hundreds who acknowledge their debt of gratitude to you. Not only is Manchester College a monument to your tireless energy and enthusiasm, but there are countless lives scattered to the four corners of the earth who can testify that your touch moulded them and made them vastly richer. I ask to be included in that number, for I owe you more than I can say.

Only eternity can reveal the magnitude of the service you have rendered to the Kingdom of God. I have always admired the deep devotion and loyalty you have given to the church, even under the most trying circumstances. As I have seen you at work for the church, you have placed it above your own convenience, above your own health and well-being, and no sacrifice was too great to make for the church of our fathers. It has been a joy to me to have a little part in working with you in the church —it has been a rare privilege. Some of the decisions of our Conference have been far-reaching in their effects —decisions that were made under your careful guidance —and the good you have accomplished there will endure long after most of the rest of us have been forgotten.

May our Father richly bless you with health, with keenness of insight and with spiritual power, that you may continue to accomplish much for the Kingdom.

Sincerely,
Signed, Edward Kintner

President Winger's interest in the college was not narrowly academic. While he expected his teachers to make good with their students and be faithful to their tasks, he gave them great latitude and freedom for outside activities, especially for activities that would result in desirable publicity for the college. One writes:

The freedom that you have given me in my field work has been highly prized. When I have gone away to meet significant groups here and there I have felt always that I had your blessing. . . . You have had during all these years a remarkable capacity to discriminate between a narrow academic point of view on the one side, and genuine scholarship associated with service to the church, the community, and the world on the other side.

While giving freedom to his faculty, President Winger was not willing that the faculty should jeopardize the good reputation of the college by teaching dangerous doctrines — especially in the Bible department. When a teacher in a course on religion proposed using a textbook which President Winger thought too modernistic he frankly objected to having the teacher use it. When reports of dangerous doctrines being taught came to him from the field or student body he made inquiry. If he found them true, he challenged the teacher and attempted to set him right.

The following letter to a Bible teacher reflects his attitude pretty accurately at near the midpoint of his presidency:

Both from reports coming to us from those without the college and from students in the college we learn that your attitude and teaching on certain subjects differs widely from the accepted views of the Church of the Brethren. . . .

That these criticisms are serious [is] indicated both by the criticism that comes from without and from your

students who indicate . . . their faith has been greatly
weakened in the Church of the Brethren, the church of
their early choice and the church that has built up and
is maintaining Manchester College.

We insist on the terms of our contract with you, "that
you exemplify in life and teachings the doctrines and
practices of the Church of the Brethren as interpreted by
her Annual Conference." We insist that this shall be
so not only in your classroom, but in private conferences
with your students as well.

. . . it is the inherent right of every people to teach
without opposition from within or without, those principles which they hold dear and hold to be true. . . . We
believe it to be the duty of every teacher, while engaged
by the college, to be true to his contract and the institution and the church that maintains it; otherwise to
sever his relations.

This was a message from the executive board,
written by the president. Only the essentials are
included. The letter was softened somewhat by
good wishes, but this is the gist of it. This expresses
his view of the matter.

Judging from all that we know about President Winger he was a sincere believer in the doctrines and practices of the church. He also believed
that a church college ought to uphold the religious
doctrines and practices of the church, as well as its
social ideals. For these he would do battle. He
believed it was the right of the church to ask for
such loyalty, and that it was his duty to enforce
it. If a teacher could not sincerely accept these doctrines and practices he should exercise his freedom
by withdrawing from the college.

It is, however, fair to say that except in the
Bible department he allowed great freedom to his

faculty. There is no evidence of interference with freedom of instruction in other departments.

SALARIES

The salaries of the faculty of Manchester in the early days were pitifully low, and have never been high. In March of 1911, the executive board of the college was authorized to contract with the faculty for the next year; namely, Otho Winger (president) at ninety dollars per month for nine months, and sixty dollars per month for the rest of the year; L. D. Ikenberry, ninety dollars per month for thirty-six weeks, and sixty dollars per month for the rest; I. B. Book at eight hundred dollars in nine equal payments; M. L. Sandifer, twelve hundred dollars in twelve equal payments; Edward Kintner, three hundred sixty dollars in nine equal payments, etc.

In September 1912 President Winger's salary was increased ten dollars per month, and L. D. Ikenberry's five dollars per month. In September of 1915, President Winger was re-elected for a three-year period at twelve hundred dollars per year. At the same time there were at least three others on the staff receiving the same amount. Other salaries ranged from seven hundred twenty to ten hundred thirty-five for nine months' service. By 1920 the president's salary had risen to twenty-two hundred dollars. Two others were receiving eighteen hundred dollars each and others ranged from nine hundred ninety to seventeen hundred forty dollars. In January of that year there was added to the salary of seven of the teachers one hundred dollars and to six others fifty dollars for the high cost of living.

By 1922 the president's salary finally rose to three thousand dollars and faculty salaries had risen correspondingly. The president's salary, however, never rose above thirty-six hundred dollars, the dean's above three thousand dollars, and top faculty salaries above twenty-seven hundred dollars for forty-one weeks' service during President Winger's administration.

It is a remarkable tribute to President Winger's ability as an administrator that he could hold together a faculty, a number of them of top-flight ability, at such low salaries. His remarkable enthusiasm and faith in the institution held them loyal to him and the college when salaries were exceedingly low. Part of this loyalty grew out of the fact that he refused to take a large salary for himself. At times his monthly salary was less than the salaries of certain of his faculty. He was always unselfish and self-sacrificing, and most generous toward others.

During depression years when students found it difficult to find enough money to go to college, President Winger confronted the faculty with the problem. The alternatives were to require cash of students and have a reduced enrollment, or to allow students who had little or no money to come and trust them to pay later. To make this possible the faculty were to contribute a certain percentage of their salaries. The faculty accepted the latter alternative and for some years returned to the college from six to ten percent of their salaries. This practice was in force at the close of his administration.

This policy of making it possible for students to come to college with little or almost no money made it possible for many to get their training who otherwise would have been unable to attend. Not all the students took seriously their obligation to the college, with the result that by 1941 there were on the books of the college practically one hundred thousand dollars in unpaid student accounts. A considerable part of this was collected with great effort but much has never been collected!

President Winger had the good fortune to have on his staff for a number of years several men who were unusually capable as public speakers. Professor J. R. Schutz went to every city and hamlet as speaker at luncheon clubs, commencements, baccalaureate services, and various other public gatherings. Only one other man in Indiana gave as many commencement addresses. Professor Schutz was a man of great charm of personality, unusually gifted as a public speaker. He won many friends for the college. Many people knew the college only through him.

A. W. Cordier, professor of history, an alumnus of the college holding a doctor's degree from the University of Chicago, was another popular speaker. He had made several trips to Europe, had studied at Geneva for a year, and had visited South America. He was an authority on international affairs and was sought after in many cities to speak to influential groups. Both these men had an interest in politics. Dr. Cordier added greatly to the reputation of the college through his lectures, and later as chairman of the Brethren Service Committee. After the close of President Winger's administration he also served in the State Department at Washington and later as the executive assistant to the Secretariat of the United Nations.

J. Oscar Winger was the fieldman for the college for many years. He was a popular and effective evangelist. He was an equally popular luncheon-club speaker. He visited hundreds of high schools and was welcomed by students and teachers alike for his inspirational addresses. He was an unselfish assistant to the president for a number of years during the latter part of Otho's presidency.

Some of the faculty members devoted their time more exclusively to the work of the church and made their contributions in that field. This was true of L. W. Shultz, W. W. Peters, R. H. Miller, and others.

Still others of the faculty at various times spoke on a lesser scale in churches, in school commencements, or elsewhere. All these public contacts added to the stature of the college in the community and the state.

Buildings and Equipment

When Otho Winger became president of the college there were four main buildings, already mentioned, on the campus. Soon after he became president the minutes of the trustee board abound with references like the following:

On motion, the Executive Committee are permitted to build a temporary gymnasium without involving the trustees financially, if possible [September 25, 1911]. . . . On motion, the Executive Committee was to take steps to enlarge the Commercial Department [March 26, 1912]. . . . On motion, it was agreed to raise at least $30,000 for the enlargement of the Ladies' Dormitory and for the erection of other buildings and to make such other improvements as the increased attendance of the college demands. And that the trustees are required to have their respective districts duly solicited for said funds [September 12, 1912]. . . . On motion, the Executive Board were instructed to enter into a contract for the purchase of three acres of land, north of the college buildings [January 14, 1913]. . . . Trustees authorize the Executive Board to erect a heating plant, estimated to cost $1500 [March 25, 1913]. . . . The Executive Board was authorized to buy seven lots adjoining the college campus for $200 [March 25, 1913]. . . . The Executive Board were authorized to erect a science and agriculture building [April 21, 1914]. . . . In September of 1915 plans were adopted to enlarge the library, and plans were to be made for enlarging the ladies' dormitory.

While this building program was going on the minutes of the board also made frequent references to the employment of fieldmen. George L. Studebaker, Manly Deeter, W. H. Burns, H. A. Studebaker, John Appleman, and S. P. Early all helped out at one time or another. Their salaries were as low as two dollars a day and traveling expenses, and in the early years never more than about eighty dollars per month. Some were solicitors for funds, some for students, and some for both. It was a period of expansion.

The first building erected in President Winger's administration was a frame gymnasium. "That seems strange," he wrote in his *Memories of Manchester*, "that a college with so little money and so small attendance should begin there; but the young folks wanted it and almost demanded it. Other colleges everywhere were building gymnasiums, and Manchester must have one to attract new students." It was a frame building, and the money for it was raised among the town merchants, the faculty, and the students. L. D. Ikenberry planned the building and the students did much of the work. The boys did the work while the girls provided the inspiration. Though the building was cheaply built and was in many ways inadequate, yet it served its purpose for a time.

In 1915 a small building was constructed which was called the science hall. Up to that time the science work was done in the basement of Bumgerdner Hall. This building was destined to be used soon for an extension practice-teaching school and later for the library. It now houses the library, the museum, and the speech and arts departments. The building was enlarged in 1926 to provide stacks for the library.

A gift from an anonymous family in 1919 made possible the purchase of a large twelve-room house one block off the campus to be used as a college hospital. The health service for students in charge of a registered nurse is now conducted from this building, and there are a number of hospital beds to care for students during temporary illnesses. Later the first floor of this building was used as a practice house for home economics majors. It has been a great blessing to the students.

In 1915 the class of 1914 donated a greenhouse as a memorial to the college; it has continued to serve the biology department of the college from that time.

A central heating plant was constructed for the college in 1913 and enlarged and rebuilt in 1939. It now contains three larger boilers, stokers, and other equipment. The whole college plant is now heated from this center.

President Winger twice enlarged Oakwood Hall, the girls' dormitory. It could accommodate about fifty girls when first built. In 1916 it was enlarged to care for about one hundred fifty girls, and then again in 1926 it was enlarged so that it now can accommodate approximately two hundred fifty. It was the hope of some that the last unit might be a separate unit, but President Winger preferred to enlarge the old dormitory and utilize one cooking establishment to supply the dining hall, and it was so!

In 1923 the Goshorn brothers of Ladoga, Indiana, made a contribution to the college which made possible the building of the cement block chemistry building, which, while unpretentious and inexpensive, has nevertheless provided the housing for many worthy medical students and research scientists under the able teachers in that department.

The two major building efforts were the administration building and the gymnasium-auditorium. It became evident by 1920 that more adequate office space and more classrooms were needed. Again it was a debate whether it should be a separate unit or a union of two already existing buildings (the Bible school building and Bumgerdner Hall) with the new building. Again, the latter plan prevailed and a very large administration building emerged. It is probably not unfair to say that President Winger loved bigness, in buildings and perhaps in number of students. This building has proved very, very useful and provides classroom space for hundreds of students as well as adequate office space for the college administrative officials.

By the mid-twenties there was pressure for a more adequate gymnasium and physical education plant, and for an enlarged auditorium. The alumni were especially interested in this. The college had had unusual success with its basketball teams and more space was needed. So a campaign was started by the alumni and others to build an alumni gymnasium and auditorium. When about sixty-five thousand dollars had been raised in cash and pledges, the plans drawn by Professor Ikenberry were submitted to various builders. When the contractors' bids were opened it was evident that the college would need about twice as much money to meet the estimated cost. So all the bids were rejected, and Professor Ikenberry, the business manager, was requested to build the building. He acted as foreman, employed men, and built the larger gymnasium-auditorium seating more than seventeen hundred people for approximately sixty-five thousand dollars. Unfortunately many of these pledges were not paid, perhaps because of depression, and the college had to use endowment funds to complete the building. Only a small share of this was later repaid by the alumni.

This building has proved exceedingly useful for the physical education program, for basketball games, for baccalaureate and commencement occasions, for college plays, and for regional conferences. In 1945 the Annual Conference of the Church of the Brethren was held there.

In 1939 President Winger and his associates also built a wing to this building as a gymnasium for girls. It is a very useful but inexpensive building. It is used for girls' physical education and for roller skating purposes.

It should also be said that during President Winger's administration the college bought the Simon Burkett house across the street from the college and another adjacent house and constructed in each six two- and three-room apartments for staff members or for married students. These have been in great demand and are very useful.

L. D. IKENBERRY

It seems fitting to say a word about L. D. Ikenberry in connection with President Winger's program of building. He was treasurer and business manager during the whole of the thirty-year period of Winger's presidency.

He was for a time professor of mathematics and astronomy. Later his teaching gave way to other responsible duties. He was a quiet, taciturn man. He knew accounting and business and had a practical knowledge of building which made him invaluable to the college. He spent much time on the campus in his office suit, often taking hold with

78

his own hands to get the work done. It is amazing how he got results.

It seems that his ability to make a dollar go a long way and his ideas about buildings for a rapidly growing college with small means fitted into the needs of Manchester and into the ideas of President Winger. For a long time they seemed an ideal pair for the building of a college. President Winger was sometimes criticized for building cheaply. To this criticism he always replied, and not infrequently with some heat, that they built as well as they could build with what means were available. If he had waited until plenty of money was on hand no college would have existed. Without an Otho Winger to raise funds there could have been no buildings at the college; but it is almost as true that without an L. D. Ikenberry there could have been no such phenomenal growth at Manchester. Each was necessary to the other, and for the period during which the writer had the privilege of working with them in intimate contact as dean and as a member of the executive board there never was a man more loyal to his chief and more co-operative than was L. D. Ikenberry; and President Winger likewise appreciated and gave recognition to the great work of Professor Ikenberry.

One must recognize the rapidity of the growth of the college and the small amount of educational sentiment among the constituency to appreciate this building program properly. At the close of President Winger's administration, instead of four buildings there were ten buildings, some of them very large, a few of them the equivalent to two or three of the earlier buildings. All save one of these were built during the first fifteen years of his presidency. It was indeed a *period of expansion*.

It is well to remember that these buildings were built without the benefit of professional architects or contractors. The contract for the boys' dormitory housing ninety-six men in 1906, after the foundation had been built, was ten thousand dollars. The administration building cost approximately one hundred thousand dollars; the gymnasium-auditorium, sixty to sixty-five thousand dollars. Every one of these buildings would at present cost from five to ten times as much as when constructed.

It seems significant that during the last fifteen years of his presidency, Dr. Winger built only the girls' gymnasium and that at low cost. It was his hope that he might build an arts building before closing his work. But in this he was doomed to disappointment and it grieved him greatly. A men's dormitory also was in his program as the next building after the arts building. His failing health and some differences of opinion as to the urgency of the arts building slowed his program.

STUDENT GROWTH

Manchester College, having very little endowment, has always been greatly dependent upon income from student fees. President Winger was aware, therefore, of the importance of a good enrollment, and this reflects itself in his diaries and his correspondence.

He was happy when he discovered that one

Trebelcock's Otho Winger, Painted in 1936

J. Oscar Winger,
Otho's Brother and
Devoted Helper

L. D. Ikenberry,
Treasurer of
Manchester College
Through Otho
Winger's Presidency

hundred twenty-five had enrolled at the opening of the first year of his presidency. From this time on the enrollment increased rapidly until in 1926 it had reached one thousand forty-five.

The growth in attendance is shown by the following table. The first one shows the total number of different students enrolled in all departments during a twelve months' period. The second table shows only the collegiate enrollment for the regular nine months' period. In 1923 the academy was closed. After that practically all the students were of collegiate rank. By comparing the two tables one discovers that the period of great growth was from about 1915 to 1926.

After that the school held a pretty steady enrollment until the Second World War. Summer school attendance fluctuated widely and was greatly affected by teacher - training requirements in Indiana.

Total Enrollment by Years in All Departments

1912-1913	328	1926-1927	1193
1913-1914	350	1927-1928	1135
1914-1915	427	1928-1929	1223
1915-1916	488	1929-1930	1067
1916-1917	556	1930-1931	1067
1917-1918	556	1931-1932	973
1918-1919	476	1932-1933	836
1919-1920	670	1933-1934	867
1920-1921	830	1934-1935	867
1921-1922	964	1935-1936	946
1922-1923	1015	1936-1937	1062
1923-1924	1050	1937-1938	1108
1924-1925	1016	1938-1939	1148
1925-1926	1045	1939-1940	1029

1940-1941	889		1945-1946	734
1941-1942	697		1946-1947	1018
1942-1943	674		1947-1948	1006
1943-1944	474		1948-1949	1049
1944-1945	502		1949-1950	1024

Summary of College Enrollment (Regular Session)
1900 - 1950

	Men	Women	Total		Men	Women	Total
1900-1901			4	1925-1926	272	359	631
1901-1902			6	1926-1927	285	379	664
1902-1903	2	0	2	1927-1928	274	363	637
1903-1904			4	1928-1929	283	353	636
1904-1905	7	3	10	1929-1930	276	345	621
1905-1906	10	1	11	1930-1931	280	331	611
1906-1907	5	3	8	1931-1932	270	341	611
1907-1908	8	3	11	1932-1933	268	332	600
1908-1909	9	8	17	1933-1934	265	318	583
1909-1910	17	4	21	1934-1935	292	300	592
1910-1911			24	1935-1936	306	330	636
1911-1912	30	17	47	1936-1937	320	362	682
1912-1913	45	29	74	1937-1938	292	367	659
1913-1914	64	35	99	1938-1939	322	367	675
1914-1915	75	41	116	1939-1940	342	320	662
1915-1916	108	45	153	1940-1941	341	297	638
1916-1917	114	92	206	1941-1942	270	281	551
1917-1918	94	89	183	1942-1943	242	298	540
1918-1919	71	68	139	1943-1944	94	267	361
1919-1920	155	125	280	1944-1945	86	301	387
1920-1921	193	148	341	1945-1946	131	339	470
1921-1922	295	285	560	1946-1947	474	348	822
1922-1923	252	235	487	1947-1948	529	302	831
1923-1924	191	297	488	1948-1949	529	311	840
1924-1925	232	343	575	1949-1950	477	327	804

It is perhaps also fair to call attention to the fact that the years of Otho Winger's presidency at

Manchester College coincided with a period of general educational growth in the United States. Especially, during the late "teens" and the twenties, immediately following World War I, there was great growth in college attendance throughout the United States. According to statistics there were enrolled in higher educational institutions in the United States in 1910 one hundred eighty-three thousand five hundred eighty-three young men and women; in 1920 there were five hundred ninety-seven thousand eight hundred eighty; by 1930 there were one million one hundred thousand seven hundred thirty-seven; and in 1940, one million four hundred ninety-four thousand two hundred three. This is the great period of expansion at Manchester also. From about 1926 to 1941 the attendance at Manchester College remained practically constant. The great growth was from about 1912 to 1926.

However, during this same period other colleges in Indiana and some elsewhere in the Church of the Brethren failed to grow and some declined in size while general conditions provided the possibility of growth; yet it took energy and enthusiasm to bring about such growth.

On February 25, 1922, President Winger wrote in his diary: "This has been the greatest term in Manchester College. The enrollment reached 520. The character of the work and the amount of it makes the term a great term." And again on March 4, 1924: "We are having a great year at the College. More than 500 students are at work and I think I can truly say we never had a finer crowd of young people than we have had this year."

His optimism and enthusiasm are reflected in his diary in such expressions as:

. . . fine weather — good school.

Closing Chapel services well attended, a large class program in the afternoon, more and more people come. Hardly one-half able to get in for Commencement at 8 p.m.

More than 1000 enrolled this year. A great year.

This has been a great day at College. Everything seems to go just right.

His diary reflects the interest and enthusiasm he had regarding the enrollment. On Tuesday, September 10, 1912: "Enrollment 140." On September 7, 1914: "Busy day meeting students." On September 8: "Enrollment day, 152 the first day, two more than one year before." September 9: "Enrollment reaches 172, busy adjusting schedules." On September 12: "Enrollment reaches 186." On September 7, 1915: "Enrollment 170 first day."

On December 3, 1915, the enrollment reached two hundred fifty-seven. President Winger's father had said that he wanted to be the three-hundredth student to enroll. So on September 26, 1916, the president's diary reports: "Great Event. The three hundredth student, John M. Winger."

On September 11, 1923, he wrote: "Fall enrollment 309 first day." The next day he wrote, "Enrollment 400 today," and on the next, "Enrollment reaches 466." On April 30, 1924, he reported, "The mid-spring enrollment is complete. The largest enrollment in the history of Manchester, 621 students. A very fine class of folks." Then follow these words, "Seniors took a day off."

His enthusiasm for the enrollment never seemed to wane. His correspondence, his diaries, and his reports to the trustees abound with it, and each year he seemed to think the students were the best yet. A paragraph of a letter to H. C. Early, written September 13, 1936, is typical.

I have been wanting to write you for some time, but I have been very busy. I never had a busier August in my life. We were almost swamped with applications for folks to come to college, and now since school has opened with the largest attendance we ever had, my work is not less, for we do have a large attendance. In fact, it is most too large. Nearly 700 students are now on our grounds. Our work has never started out better.

Enlarging the Constituency

One of the great contributions of President Winger to Manchester College was the enlargement of the constituency by getting additional church districts to appoint trustees and thus become part-owners and supporters of the college.

When the church took over the college in 1901 there were five state districts that considered themselves part-owners and supporters of Manchester. They were Southern Illinois, Northern Indiana, Middle Indiana, Southern Ohio, and Northwestern Ohio. On April 13, 1915, the trustees of the college passed a motion providing that the secretary should write to each elder in charge of a church in Northeastern Ohio for permission to canvass the church under his charge. Then on September 14, 1915, resolutions were adopted inviting the districts of Northeastern Ohio and Michigan each to elect a trustee to the college. President Winger then visited these district meetings and persuaded each to elect a trustee. Southern Indiana also had elected a trustee; now all of Indiana, Ohio, and Michigan was considered Manchester College territory—both for student solicitation and solicitation for funds. In the Michigan district conference a representative from another Brethren college was present; but he gave way to the appeal from Otho Winger and Manchester secured the territory.

Mount Morris College's special field consisted of Illinois, Iowa, Wisconsin, North Dakota, and Minnesota, though it earlier also drew many students from Indiana and Ohio. It had had able leadership in such men as J. G. Royer, J. E. Miller, and others and graduated many able students such as Wilbur Stover, A. J. Brumbaugh, L. S. Shively, J. S. Noffsinger, A. R. Eikenberry, and many others. E. S. Young and his brother, S. S. Young, who helped found Manchester College, came from Mount Morris College.

But of late years Mount Morris had had difficult times. It changed presidents every few years through the twenties. At various times there was much talk of closing the school. At one time in the twenties the trustees actually announced the closing of the college, and then reconsidered. In 1931 a fire took one of their main buildings. Then it seemed that they would surely close the school. But they rebuilt and went on.

During all this time President Winger played a very shrewd and diplomatic part. When he was called on for advice by the Mount Morris administration he offered helpful suggestions; when asked whether they should close, he always replied that that was for the trustees of Mount Morris to decide. At the same time he offered to be of any assistance he could. He assured them of his goodwill and good wishes and was very sympathetic and helpful in all his relations to them. His letters to them reveal a very gracious spirit.

When the fire occurred in 1931, the members of the General Educational Board of the Church of the Brethren, under the chairmanship of Dr. C. C. Ellis, offered their services to the Mount Morris trustees and met with them. In view of the oft-repeated suggestion of closing Mount Morris it seemed to them that it was unwise to rebuild. Otho Winger did not attend this meeting. He had just had an automobile accident.

In view of the long-time friendliness of Otho Winger toward Mount Morris and the proximity of Manchester College it is not strange that when the trustees of Mount Morris decided to merge their college with another they turned to Manchester. Mount Morris merged her institutional identity with Manchester and deposited her records there. The funds of the college were to be divided and the territory was left to a vote by church districts to join any other college territory it chose. The outcome was that the District of Northern Illinois and Wisconsin joined up with Manchester, and Iowa, Minnesota, and North Dakota with McPherson College.

The wisdom and diplomacy of Otho Winger had now won for Manchester all the area of the Old

Northwest Territory as its geographic constituency among Brethren churches, a membership of about fifty-one thousand, one of the largest in the church.

SOCIAL IDEALS

As has been noted elsewhere, Otho Winger was greatly devoted to the Church of the Brethren. He knew her history, he believed in her doctrines, he admired her leaders, and he accepted and upheld her social ideals. In his personal life he exemplified her teaching on the simple life. He stressed the virtues of purity, honesty, industry, thrift, generosity, and democracy.

It was his belief that the college should reflect and support these social ideals. He was strongly opposed to dancing and card playing; drinking was not tolerated and smoking was discouraged. Through all the thirty years he stood for those ideals, and, while tolerant of the weakness of youth, he was as adamant as Gibraltar in support of the ideals.

While he believed the college should uphold the ideals and doctrines of the Church of the Brethren and serve the needs of that church, yet he was most tolerant of other faiths and made every effort to welcome to the campus any Protestant, Catholic, or Jewish students. In some cases he personally took his car and drove students of the Catholic faith to near-by cities so that they could participate in the Mass. While he welcomed those of other faiths, he required that they conform to the social ideals of the college.

It soon became evident that there were many

parents in other churches who appreciated the conservative social ideals of Manchester, and were dissatisfied with those of their own colleges. As it became evident that students from other denominations were getting equal treatment with Brethren at Manchester, many parents sent their children to the college. This was especially true of some of the pastors of other churches in north-central Indiana.

Manchester was fortunately situated in its part of Indiana. There were for many years no strong competing Protestant colleges very near it. In a strip of fifty or more miles across Indiana from east to west no fully standardized Protestant college existed. Here was a rich field in which Manchester could operate. The college had for a number of years been a strong teacher-training institution. Into this open field in north-central Indiana, Manchester College now sent hundreds of teachers for the public schools. From this same area the college drew many capable students.

President Winger appreciated this constituency and did all he could to serve these people and cultivate their goodwill. He and his brother, J. O., along with Professor Schutz and Dr. Cordier, were popular in teachers' circles and gave many commencement addresses to the high schools — large and small—in Indiana. The contribution of the other faculty members already mentioned aided in cultivating this clientele.

It has been noted that Manchester was more of an academy, commercial college, and Bible school than a real college when Otho Winger became president. There never were more than three college graduates until 1914. As high schools came to be more prevalent in small towns and rural areas, young people took their preparatory work there, rather than at college.

At Manchester, however, the academy continued until 1923. For a number of years it was necessary to have a separate administration and faculty for the academy in order to receive accreditment for the college department. Professor L. W. Shultz and Professor L. J. Yoder served as principals of the academy for some years. But along about 1920 or 1921 the academy began to decline. By 1923 it had been reduced to forty students and was closed at the end of that year. However, the college continued to give diplomas for short courses in teacher-training, secretarial, or commercial work for a time.

The college was always interested in preparing young people to teach. Manchester early came to be known as a strong teacher-training institution. For some time the head of the department was known as the dean of education. Later, education came to be considered one of the regular departments of the college, but continued a strong department with seven or eight full-time teachers. For many years, from sixty to seventy percent of the graduates of the college have become teachers. In some counties surrounding the college more than half of the public school teachers have attended Manchester College. The town school, the Chester Township schools, Wabash, and Warsaw provide practice-teaching facilities in good school systems in which students may serve an apprenticeship. Thousands of our alumni are elementary teachers, high school teachers, high school principals, superintendents of schools, college teachers, deans, and college presidents.

ACCREDITMENT

Manchester College was for many years not certified by any of the regional or national accrediting agencies. It managed to get full recognition by the state departments of education in Indiana and surrounding states from which the college drew most of its students, and for which it trained teachers.

It took constant effort to keep up with the rising requirements of the state for standardization. To this need President Winger was very alert and he succeeded in this effort. All the while the permanence and the stability of the institution was being jeopardized by its lack of recognition in the North Central Association, the accrediting agency for this region.

President Winger did not seem to be in a hurry to make application for admission to the association; at least so it seemed to the author, who was then dean. The president was aware of certain shortcomings of the college and perhaps did not want to make an unsuccessful application. But finally he made a heroic effort, made arrangements to handle the finances of the college so as to make the best showing, increased the endowment, and made the application during the school year 1931-1932.

The surveyors were Dr. A. J. Cline of Ohio State University and Dr. Walter A. Payne of the

University of Chicago. President Winger had a great deal to say in some of his writings about the difference between these two men. One seemed practical and nontechnical, the other almost purely academic in his approach. President Winger liked the man who talked to faculty, students, businessmen, and alumni about the college rather than the one who applied formal standards to the measurements of the college.

In the spring of 1932, the spring of the merger with Mount Morris College, Manchester was accredited with the proviso that there be an annual review until standards would be more fully met. The following improvements were called for:

(1) Increased endowment of fifty thousand dollars per year until minimum standards are met.

(2) Reduction of the number of offerings and catalog listings in certain departments.

(3) Revision of curricula to make more effective use of time of students and faculty.

(4) Increases of library purchases and improvement of teaching methods.

(5) Progressive increases of faculty salaries.

(6) Catalog to be more clearly written, padding and repetitions removed.

(7) A more competent assistant for women's physical education.

A flood of letters reached the president on achieving recognition by the North Central Association, many of them personally complimenting him for his great achievements for the college. After a re-inspection or two the college was recognized without further annual inspections.

On January 13, 1926, the trustees of the college adopted a lengthy resolution to be sent to the churches of Indiana, Ohio, and Michigan—a resolution which is almost certainly the product of President Winger's pen. It was at the midpoint of his presidency, and so fully defines his position on a number of issues that it is included here.

We your representatives and trustees of Manchester College hereby desire to address you in the interest of this institution.

We are pleased to report a most successful year. The student attendance has kept well above the 650 mark all year. Not only with the number in attendance but with the character of the work, we are well pleased. But with so large a number of young people to direct into proper lines of conduct and usefulness, the responsibility is very great.

The current finances of the year show as good condition as ever in the history of the school. Yet the ever increasing expense of properly providing for so many students and meeting standard conditions, makes the problem of finance as great as ever.

Now in the realization of our opportunities and responsibility, realizing the many problems and dangers in modern education and the great task of financing an institution, we present to you the following:

First: the trustees renew their purpose and determination to maintain in teaching and conduct of the college the fundamental principles of the Bible, believing it to be the Word of God, our only rule of faith and practice. We pledge anew our allegiance to God and His Word, to Jesus Christ our Redeemer and Savior, and to the Holy Spirit who has spoken to men through the Word, and through whose direction alone we expect to do all things well.

93

We pledge anew our loyalty and allegiance to the Church and to society, desiring above all other things to prepare men and women for the largest service possible. To this end we are not only concerned that there be proper teaching, but also that there be proper training in living. We are insisting that both students and teachers maintain high standards of morality and conduct and that we may be saved from many of the popular follies of the day. We commend the management and faculty in their efforts to maintain such good conditions.

We renew our request to our members and churches that there be given the largest financial help possible. To properly care for our growing needs, not only must there be new buildings, we must also use some of our endowment to maintain proper standardization. We commend the work of our promotion committee and urge your generous response to their presentation and appeals.

Realizing the value of the most efficient help possible, we believe that our trustee board should be increased to twelve members. We have nine at present—seven elected directly by the churches, one by the alumni and the President of the institution who is a member, ex-officio. We recommend that the trustees' body be allowed to nominate three trustees at large to be chosen for their special fitness and helpfulness, all of whom shall be members of the Church of the Brethren, these trustees to serve three years, except the ones first chosen who shall serve one, two, and three years respectively. These nominations shall be confirmed by the districts of the churches, and no trustee shall serve unless he shall receive the unanimous approval of all the districts.

ORGANIZATION OF THE COLLEGE

We have seen that when President Winger took over his duties as president, the organization of the college was very meager. He was president and L. D. Ikenberry was treasurer. There was usually

94

a fieldman. George L. Studebaker functioned for a while as business manager and field secretary. His duties as business manager seemed to be to help look after the supplies for the dormitories, and perhaps to supervise some up-keep on the campus; later men like Manly Deeter, C. A. Wright, G. A. Snider, Edson Ulrey, and E. B. Bagwell served as finance and field secretary. For the last eighteen or twenty years his chief student recruiting and soliciting officer was his brother, J. O. Winger.

For a number of years after becoming president, Winger had an executive board made up of L. D. Ikenberry and a few of the trustees and himself. In 1919 the dean became an advisory member of the executive board, and in January of 1920 a regular member. From about 1920 to 1927, when Dean Schwalm left Manchester to go to McPherson as president, the executive board consisted of Otho Winger, L. D. Ikenberry, G. A. Snider, Edson Ulrey, and V. F. Schwalm. This body had power to act for the trustees between meetings. Their acts were usually approved when the trustees met. Important issues of a policy-forming nature were usually left for the trustees to determine. But the determination of budgetary matters and a host of routine matters arising in the operation of the college were decided by this board.

In 1933 the executive board consisted of Otho Winger, president of the college; L. D. Ikenberry, treasurer and business manager; Carl W. Holl, dean of the college; J. G. Meyer, dean of education; Edward Kintner, secretary of the faculty; and G. A. Snider, secretary of the board of trustees. This body came to have a great deal of power and was very influential in determining school policy. Robert L. Kelley, secretary of the Association of American Colleges, who made a survey of all Brethren colleges in 1933, says, "Most of the work directing the institution is referred to the Executive Board of six appointed for three years by the Board of Trustees."

Robert Kelley further says of the executive board that meetings are held monthly and at such other times as the president deems necessary. The secretary of the faculty brings to this board any decisions of the faculty which may have to do with its work. In fact, the executive board deals with almost every activity of the college, including recommendations of faculty members to the trustees, salaries, care of plant, and employment of helpers. It is responsible for many duties usually assigned to the president. No faculty member hesitates to express himself to anyone on the board with respect to any question. The board's control over appointments and financial matters brings the faculty in close contact with administrative problems and has resulted in an unusually fine "esprit de corps."

To continue Kelley's observations further:

The president of the college, while having a general interest and concern for the entire institution is immediately responsible for the discipline and general welfare of students, for relations with parents, oversight of field work including student solicitation and financial promotion.

When the examining committee of the North Central Association had surveyed the college in

1932, one of the elements of strength noted by the examiners was described thus:

The assignment of executive functions to a resident Executive Board, made up of officers who teach in the college tends to result in constant authoritative action and in intimate identification of the entire faculty with the management of the institution.

In Robert Kelley's survey, made the next year after the North Central survey, he commends the executive board setup by saying:

The close cooperation of the Board of Trustees and the faculty through the medium of the Executive Board composed with one exception of faculty members but appointed by the Board of Trustees, is an exemplification not often found in college management of what may be today called progressive education. As a matter of fact the impulse came historically from the necessity of having the college managed by educational men. All this raises some very interesting questions as to the real functions of the Board of Trustees and of the faculty as a group. Perhaps Manchester has a message in this area of college administration somewhat different from the traditional American message. The student government organization cooperates also with the Executive Board.

The trustees of Manchester were early elected for three-year periods by church districts in their district conferences. They were usually ministers, usually men of some strength and leadership in their districts. Jacob Coppock, L. W. Teeter, John Calvin Bright, Daniel Garver, and others were men of considerable strength and influence in their day. But not many of them had much experience in educational matters. Their selection was out of the control of the college except as nominating committees would consult with the president or as he might make a telling suggestion at the proper places.

On January 8, 1923, the alumni were assigned a trustee, elected from among their own group, and the president was given membership on the board; and in 1926, as we have seen, the president of the college suggested the election of three trustees-at-large, to be nominated by the board of trustees and approved by the districts. All were to be members of the Church of the Brethren, and all were to serve three years when appointed. A trustee so appointed was to receive the unanimous approval of all the districts. In 1931 the trustees-at-large were increased to four by adding a resident of North Manchester and the alumni were allowed to nominate a second trustee, one to be a woman. During the later years the trustees included not only ministers, but manufacturers, school principals, teachers, and men of affairs; many of them were college graduates and men of broad experience.

On January 9, 1917, two standing committees of the trustees of the board were formed: (1) a finance committee to audit the books and direct the investment of the funds, and (2) a visiting committee who were to visit the college once a year to study the moral and religious condition of the college.

These committees functioned for perhaps a dozen years, and then were allowed to lapse. An employed professional auditor later audited the books, and a local committee consisting of the treasurer and the finance secretary made investments. The visitors functioned for a while, giving encouraging reports of the moral and spiritual condition of the college. The General Educational Board of the church in some measure fulfilled the duties of this committee in later years.

During President Winger's administration the trustees usually met three times a year and later only two times a year except for rare occasions when especially called. Sometimes these meetings were for only a few hours. The trustees being busy men far removed from the college, and engaged in full-time occupations, it was difficult for them to give the college enough time to get into its problems. Furthermore, they had great confidence in the president and trusted his judgment implicitly and so followed his leadership.

Usually they heard the reports of the president, the dean, and the treasurer and the report of the work of the executive committee and did the necessary work brought to their attention, then returned to their homes.

Then, too, the executive board having been entrusted with the responsibility of operating the college, to them many problems were referred. On occasions when building campaigns or endowment campaigns were put on, they gave consideration to these matters. They were not nonentities in any sense, but they did not assume active responsibility in the operation of the college.

There have been, however, some exceptions to this. In the twenties there were some meetings that indicate the consideration of a long list of business items. This is also true at times in the late thirties.

On February 14, 1939, the executive board was enlarged by the addition of Dr. A. W. Cordier and Professor A. R. Eikenberry. The board now consisted of eight: the president, the dean, the head of the department of education, the secretary of the faculty, the secretary of the board of trustees, and two other faculty members.

In the minutes of the board of trustees and the president's correspondence during the period of a few years there is evidence of some rough sailing affecting trustees, faculty, and students, probably growing out of misunderstandings and differences of opinion on matters of school policy and matters of discipline affecting both faculty and students. Because of the ill-health of the president and some other internal conditions in the institution it was no longer possible for him to keep things completely under control.

In his last annual report to the trustees in January of 1941, President Winger wrote as follows regarding the administrative setup and the authority and responsibility of the president:

There is one thing I feel like saying. Manchester College has a unique method of directing the school in what is known as our Executive Board. There was an Executive Board when I first became president, but the present Executive Board is much larger and quite different from that. When Dr. Klein was here as one of the inspectors for the North Central Association, he observed our method of the Executive Board and talked to me about it. He was very much interested. He wrote up an article in the "Journal of Higher Education" about our plan. He said it was most unique and asked me if I was happy working under such a condition. For the most part I have been very much pleased with it; and yet those responsible for the direction of the school must understand what it means. I have looked upon it as that of a president and his cabinet, in which the president consults with capable members, gets their contributions and together they decide on what is best for the school. Looked at in this way, I consider it quite a success. However, if it should come to mean that the president of the college is only one-seventh or one-ninth of the head of the institution, that every other member of the Executive Board has equal authority and responsibility, then the situation becomes intolerable for the president and a source of weakness for the government of the institution. I am making this statement for the benefit of the man who succeeds me.

As long as an executive committee, constituted as the above was, has confidence in and accepts the leadership of the president both as to policy and in dealing with matters of detail as to faculty and students, such a plan can succeed. As soon as for any reason whatever the executive board ceases to follow his leadership, and the president becomes subservient to members of the executive committee, then his leadership is thwarted. Either he is the chief executive or he is not. President Winger was correct in his analysis of the situation. It is true that in the multitude of counsel there is wisdom, but, to quote Lloyd George, "you cannot conduct a war with a Sanhedrin," and we might add, "Nor a college."

President Winger appointed his first dean of the college in 1917. For ten years this position was held by V. F. Schwalm. When he resigned in 1927 to become president of McPherson College, Dr. Carl W. Holl, head of the chemistry department, was made dean and retained this position through the remainder of President Winger's administration.

The deanship of Manchester began in a small

way, but because of the frequent and sometimes prolonged absences of the president it grew to be an office of great influence and power in the institution. Dr. Holl exercised great influence among students and alumni in the office. In 1928 the first dean of men was appointed in the person of Dr. C. S. Morris, of the physics department, who was later succeeded by A. R. Eikenberry. Many of the duties of looking after housing, student employment and social affairs once looked after by President Winger were assumed by the dean of men.

The first dean of women was appointed in 1925. Della Lehman held this office for two years, and then asked for a year's leave of absence. Miss Alice Doner was appointed to fill the position during Miss Lehman's absence, and since Miss Lehman did not return Miss Doner held the position during the remainder of President Winger's administration. Many of the usual duties relating to women's housing, counseling, and discipline were taken over by that office.

For a number of years the college also had a dean of education. From 1919 until about 1938 that title was used to designate the office of the head of the department of education. He served as head of the department, kept contact with the state department of education, supervised practice-teaching work, and signed teachers' applications for certification. The position was held by Dr. W. W. Peters and after that by Dr. J. G. Meyer. The title has been discontinued but the head of the department continues to perform many of the functions.

The first registrar was employed by the college

in 1922 in the person of Cora Wise. For a little while she was also the acting dean of women but soon gave up the latter office. This position she held until 1947, and instituted a sound system of record keeping for Manchester College which has received considerable acclaim. The first engineer reported was in 1914, in the person of O. L. Replogle. The first full-time secretary to the president was employed in 1924, in the person of Clara Harper, later missionary to Africa. In 1936, President Winger employed a full-time physician for the college, Dr. Lucille Carman, who remained with the college through the remainder of his administration.

In 1929 the trustees of the college, at the president's suggestion, formed the Manchester College Foundation and Holding Company. The purpose of the company was to hold and manage all real estate held by the college, to receive all income from auxiliary enterprises conducted by the college, and to pay new receipts to the college as income for the operation of the college. All annuity contracts were turned to the holding company to be paid by them; in that way the endowment funds of the college would not be encumbered by annuity payment obligations. This was evidently in preparation for North Central Association inspection. After the North Central Association had changed its plan of accreditation the company was discontinued, thus simplifying the financial operations of the college.

President Winger was not one to sit down and write carefully designed organizational plans. When he came face to face with a need, he met it in what seemed to him the best way possible. Some of his helpers felt the need of carefully prepared blueprints of organization, but he was either too busy doing things to undertake writing such a plan or else was disinclined to work under such a formal program.

REGIONAL EDUCATIONAL BOARD

During the latter part of President Winger's administration he arranged for a regional educational board outside the trustee board within the region; it corresponded somewhat to the General Educational Board of the total Church of the Brethren. The function of the regional board was never very clear to the writer and he has reason to believe that it was not to the members of the board. It is likely that they were to promote educational sentiment in the region and especially for the college.

WINGER AND CHAPEL

At the time of the Silver Anniversary celebration held at Manchester College in 1936, in honor of the twenty-fifth year of Otho Winger's presidency, it was said that if you were to ask any student of the past twenty-five years with what he would associate President Winger most closely, he would certainly answer, "The chapel." This is probably a correct observation.

Chapel has always held an important place in the life of Manchester. At the beginning of the Winger administration there was a daily chapel service about 9:30 in the morning for about a half-hour. Later the schedule was reduced to four chapels a week, and still later to three. Chapel attendance was required and student monitors took the roll. Frequent absence resulted in demerit marks and affected the student's standing in the school, along with other forms of misconduct. The president was generous in excusing Roman Catholic students from chapel if they asked for exemption on religious grounds. Those doing practice teaching and those who worked were excused. A student might be absent a few times each term without demerit.

Chapel was essentially a religious service. It consisted of a hymn or two, Scripture reading and prayer, and often a sermonette or short talk. Sometimes the program consisted chiefly of music, and in later years of other varied programs.

Usually the president or a member of the faculty led in worship and gave the talk. Occasionally, a pastor from one of the Brethren churches, a trustee, or some friend of the college was brought in to speak. Once in a while some noted speaker appeared, such as the state superintendent, the governor of the state, S. Parkes Cadman, or Bishop McDowell.

For many years the chapel was distinctly the president's service. He always presided when on the campus and often spoke. Here he was master and at his best. His dominant personality, strong voice, quick wit, and contagious enthusiasm gave him an unchallenged leadership for many years.

His chapel talks usually were based on some well-known Scripture passages: the Ten Commandments, the First Psalm, the Sermon on the Mount, the parable of the sower, the parable of the foolish virgins, the Lord's Prayer, the story of the prodigal son, the power of goodness, the Kingdom of God, the economy of time.

A number of these are printed in his book, *Memories of Manchester*. One reading them gets the impression of plain, good, common-sense advice. But the printed page gives little idea of their strength when spoken by a man with such evident sincerity and power, one who was devoted to the welfare of the students.

But his speeches were not the best part of his contribution to chapel. His witticisms, his quick repartee, his ability to turn an announcement or a bit of news into an enthusiasm-producing occasion were remarkable. He was master of the art of using chapel as an agency for the promotion of school spirit, and of "pepping up" drooping spirits. Visitors were recognized, successes in school activities were cited, alumni success was announced, progress in the development of the college was noted—and all in all, he made chapel a forum for unifying and promoting the welfare of the college.

But it was not always sunshine. Sometimes when there had been grave breaches of conduct, or if things did not seem to go well, he could scold. On occasion he could make a scathing denunciation of wrongdoing that would make the stoutest heart quake. After some boys had given a false fire alarm one night, and had called people from their beds, his condemnation was bitter—and it didn't happen again! When grave offenses against school standards or commonly accepted standards of morality occurred, as they occasionally did, he was severe in his condemnation.

In the later years of his presidency, he shared the chapel with others. Monday was the president's day. On Wednesday the dean planned the chapel, often using visiting Kiwanis speakers; on Thursday the program was prepared by the religious life committee of the faculty. On Friday the program was of a miscellaneous nature and often consisted of student programs.

It could probably be safely said that no one influence at Manchester lingers on in the minds of the alumni as a precious memory to which they look back with as much appreciation as does chapel. Hundreds of alumni have spoken of it. Those who enjoyed it while there continue to look back to the memory with fondness. And even many who resented the requirement while in college expressed their appreciation in later years. The following from an alumni letter to President Winger is not unusual: "I would like to hear some Chapel services again, even though I was one who used to pass them up so much. A person never knows how much of the good things . . . they pass over until they are gone. Do older people make the same mistakes?"

It was with students then as later, for when a lad came back from World War II after a period in college, he said, "Never give up chapel, especially Wednesday's chapel. It is the one thing of college I remembered in the midst of the war." Wednesday's chapel in his day was the formal worship chapel.

Otho Winger as a Churchman

Otho Winger embodied in his personality an unusual combination of qualities. He was a successful educator, an influential churchman, and a practical man of affairs. One finds it difficult to know which of these attributes was dominant in his life. His was an integrated personality with the various abilities remarkably well balanced.

We have seen that he was interested in the church and her activities and became a member when just a lad. He was active in Sunday-school work in his teens. He was elected to the deacon's office by his church on September 26, 1896. In the Church of the Brethren of that day it was the custom of the church to extend a call to a man to become a minister of the church by a vote of the membership. If he likewise felt the call he accepted the invitation and was duly installed in that office. Otho Winger was called to the ministry on April 9, 1897, when he was nineteen and one-half years of age. He was advanced to the eldership of the church November 12, 1910, when he was thirty-three years of age.

As noted elsewhere, during his boyhood he took a keen interest in visiting the sick and in the active program of the church. When he was eighteen years of age he went to Annual Conference at Decatur,

Illinois, and met J. G. Royer, the popular president of Mount Morris College, and L. T. Holsinger, who was then active in helping start Manchester College. His interest in the leaders of the church never ceased from that time forward.

He early manifested an unusual interest in older people, especially in the older leaders of the church. We have already referred to his interest in Elder Stephen Ulrey, an influential elder in Middle Indiana, with whom Otho spent time talking about matters pertaining to the church. He seemed to enjoy in a special way his friendship and association with the older churchmen of his day. In his files are letters to and from many of them. His office walls at college were covered with pictures of such outstanding leaders as D. L. Miller, L. T. Holsinger, L. W. Teeter, Jacob Coppock, I. D. Parker, D. B. Garber, J. G. Royer, J. H. Moore, H. C. Early, and others. In fact, collecting pictures of older people, especially those who attained a great age, was almost a hobby with him. His interest in these old people endeared him to many of them.

The first church work of Otho Winger was naturally done in the local church at Cart Creek, where he was Sunday-school teacher, Sunday-school superintendent, deacon, and later, minister. At college he was active in the Bible Society, which was a religious equivalent of the literary societies in that day and gave excellent experience in public speaking and various forms of self-expression. According to Alice King Ebey, he soon became one of its most active and influential members. Soon, too, according to his own words, he was "filling appointments almost every Sunday somewhere besides a growing schedule of appointments during the week." These, he said, kept him busy. He was becoming known as a capable young preacher and leader.

Between 1907, when he began to teach at Manchester College, and 1911, when he became president of the college, he was preaching in the churches, participating in varied religious activities, and broadening his interest and influence in the church in general. The records of his life for this period are meager, but judging from the way he was suddenly called to larger fields of usefulness soon after this, and from the extensive correspondence he engaged in throughout his life, this must also have been going on then.

He was in his early thirties, with a strong, vigorous body. His energies seemed exhaustless; his face was animated and friendly. His enthusiasm was contagious. His interest in people was outgoing and every contact seemed to make friends for him and for the cause he represented. His frank, open, direct address and his completely integrated personality inspired confidence. Old and young alike believed in him and trusted him.

In the Church of the Brethren the next organizational unit above the local church is the district. Indiana has three districts and Otho Winger lived in what was called the District of Middle Indiana. Above the district is the general church, whose annual business session is called the Annual Conference. This has come to be a great mass meeting for inspirational addresses and a meeting of delegates from the districts and from the churches for the transaction of business.

One of the first district offices held by Otho Winger was that of district Sunday-school secretary. This position he filled for several terms. Afterwards he served a number of times as moderator of the district conference. Later in life, as he became involved in the various offices of the Annual Conference, he declined to serve as district moderator in deference to younger men of the district.

Otho Winger began attending Annual Conference (the general conference of the church) at an early age and did not miss a single Conference from 1911 to 1936, and only two or three after that until his death in 1946. His activities soon gave evidence that he was a close student of both men and movements in the church and that he was observing the parliamentary procedures carefully.

From 1911 to 1915 and from about 1920 to 1941 he was a member of the General Educational Board of the church. This brought him in touch with some of her most capable educational leaders such as M. G. Brumbaugh, D. W. Kurtz, C. C. Ellis, Paul Bowman, and H. C. Early. More will be said of his work on this board in a later chapter.

In 1912 he was elected to the General Mission Board. At this time it was the most powerful and the most influential board of the church. It was powerful in part because of the men who served on it: D. L. Miller, author, traveler, church father; H. C. Early, dignified Southern church statesman of rare powers as a preacher and presiding officer; J. J. Yoder, wise counselor, successful businessman, far-seeing leader; Charles D. Bonsack, great-hearted, gracious, sympathetic friend, preacher; and A. P. Blough, long-time successful pastor of a great rural church at Waterloo, Iowa. These men were giants in the church of their day.

The General Mission Board was powerful also because it was the oldest board of the church, it was about the only board that had any money to spend, and missions were the chief current interest of the church. This interest was due in part to the work of such men as Wilbur Stover, Frank Crumpacker, J. M. Blough, S. N. McCann, Adam Ebey, Alice King Ebey, and others of their contemporaries and their successors.

Otho Winger served on the Mission Board for thirty-one years. During the first twelve years H. C. Early was chairman. Otho Winger succeeded him and for sixteen years was its chairman. A few years before the termination of his service on the board he resigned the chairmanship in favor of Rufus D. Bowman, in whom he had the greatest confidence.

For many years the name of Otho Winger was inseparably connected with foreign missions in the church. His interest in and his service to missions are too great and many-sided to be included in this general discussion but will be dealt with in another part of this chapter.

Another office to which he was elected was that of reading clerk of the Annual Conference. The Annual Conference then had three important officers: the moderator, the reading clerk, and the writing clerk. He was first elected reader in 1915. He was again elected reader in 1917 and still again in 1919. His strong, clear voice, his distinct, rapid reading, and his alert mind made him an excellent reader. During each of these three years, H. C. Early was the moderator. This afforded an excellent opportunity for Winger to play the role of an understudy, for Early was one of the most masterful moderators the church had produced up to that time.

In 1921 Otho Winger was first elected as moderator of Annual Conference at Hershey, Pennsylvania. He showed himself such a master at this task that he was re-elected five more times during the next thirteen years. He served as moderator in 1923 at Calgary, Alberta; in 1925 at Winona Lake, Indiana; in 1928 at La Verne, California; in 1931 at Colorado Springs, Colorado; and in 1934 at Ames, Iowa.

It was a rule of Annual Conference that officers of the meeting could not succeed themselves, and at some time in the 1920's a rule was passed which provided that one could not serve as moderator more than once in three years. It is an interesting observation that Otho Winger was reading clerk in 1915, 1917, and 1919, and moderator in 1921, 1923, 1925, 1928, 1931, and 1934, which is probably as often as the rules would have permitted him to be an elected officer of the Conference in that period from 1915 to 1934.

In 1917 Otho Winger, J. H. Longenecker, and George L. Studebaker were appointed on a committee to revise the minutes of Annual Conference, the rules governing the church. Previous publications in 1898 and 1907 had indicated the minutes in force up to 1907. The task of the committee was to eliminate minutes of a historical and therefore of a temporary character and minutes in which Conference made no ruling but referred matters to some board or committee and "to leave out all decisions that have been repealed or superseded by other decisions." This proved a long, tedious task. Otho Winger was chairman of this committee, and, as one who saw them at work, the author would conclude that he probably did the lion's share of the work.

Many matters had to go back to the Conference for actual decision. The product of their effort was then published as the *Revised Minutes of Annual Conference* in 1922.

H. C. Early was a great moderator of Conference. The Virginian was tall, erect, stern-visaged, and dignified. He looked the part of a Roman senator. Many felt he looked like the pictures of Stonewall Jackson or Robert E. Lee. He was clear-headed, firm, authoritative, and statesmanlike in outlook. He was born to lead.

Otho Winger was of medium height; he was broad shouldered, stocky, short necked, and compactly built. His voice was strong and penetrating. His manner was informal, his mental processes rapid. He was quick to comprehend a situation and to see the significance and the various ramifications of any issue. He was eager to be fair to all sides in a debate and was highly pleased when those who lost an issue admitted that he had been fair. He had a keen sense of humor and was quick at repartee.

Few presiding officers could lead a large parliamentary body through such a long docket of business in so short a time. His familiar voice saying, "Are there objections? I hear none. The clerk will read," still rings in the ears of those who sat in the audience while he presided.

During recent years no other man in the Church of the Brethren was so often elected to the moderatorship of the church. One naturally asks why he was so often called to this task. In some measure this always escapes any attempt at analysis.

If one should venture reasons they would perhaps be these: He was honest and sincere and had through a number of years won the confidence of the church people. He was friendly and winsome in his ways and made friends wherever he went. He knew the church, her leaders, and her problems, and he knew the feelings, the prejudices, the convictions, and the desires of the common church people. On most issues he found himself on the side of the conservative majority in the church. He was poised, alert, clear minded, and eminently just. He moved the business of the Conference with becoming dispatch. People appreciated the efficiency with which he handled a meeting.

While making this study the writer sent a letter to some of Otho Winger's contemporaries asking what were the elements of his strength which led to his repeated re-election as moderator? Their answers, though varied, could be listed somewhat as follows:

1. His evident faith in and devotion to the church.

2. His outstanding, dominant personality. He

was positive and forceful. He looked and talked like a leader.

3. His understanding of human nature and especially of the heartbeat of the common man. He loved the people.

4. His intuitive judgment, that was quick and accurate.

5. His evident honesty and fairness, which led people to trust him.

6. His self-confident, poised approach to a problem.

The first time Otho Winger served as moderator at Annual Conference he addressed the delegates at the beginning of the Conference. This speech is included because it reveals the spirit that characterized him as a presiding officer. The address is simple and direct, and tended to create a sense of responsibility in his hearers.

Dear brethren and sisters: We have met in the business session of our great Annual Conference of our beloved Fraternity. A delegate body like this stands in a class almost by itself among religious assemblies. A body of delegates more representative of the people they serve could hardly be imagined. Every organized congregation of our Brotherhood, however small that congregation may be, is entitled to at least one delegate to this meeting. Not only is every part of our Brotherhood represented, but every class of our people, if we may speak of all classes being represented, for here our brethren and sisters, old and young, rich and poor, college man and laborer, bishop and laymen, are sitting side by side, standing on an equality, as far as the voting power and deliberation of this meeting is concerned, and all are working together for the one great cause that we love. It is a great privilege to be a member of this body.

There is a great work to do. Here we are to formulate plans and methods of work for one hundred thousand people. Here we are to select the leaders of the activities of our church, and these activities reach to the farthest corners of the earth. These decisions today, and what we do here, affect the lives and interests of thousands and multiplied thousands of people, and generations yet unborn will be affected by what we do. Here we attempt to reduce to a working harmony, at least, differences of practice and to some extent, differences of doctrine. It is a great privilege to sit as a delegate in a body like this; it is likewise a great responsibility, for when we consider the number of persons affected and the vital issues that may be touched, it is a great responsibility to speak and to vote in this meeting. Surely, no one is entitled to sit here who has any selfish motives in view. Surely no one is entitled to sit here who is not willing to subordinate selfish or local interests to the greatest interest of the Kingdom of God. Surely no one is entitled today, or is qualified today, to sit in this body who is not willing at this hour to submit himself or herself to the direction of the Holy Spirit, that he may cleanse our thought, our feeling, our will, that he may enlighten us, that he may direct this meeting. I am sure that whatever officials may have been provided, we want the Holy Spirit to moderate and to direct and to instruct us in this meeting. I am very glad that we are united as we are; a body of people more united than this, perhaps could hardly be found. Here is the great declaration of principles and purposes which every delegate on the Standing Committee, which every delegate of this voting body has read and has accepted. If you will read the contents of this declaration of principles and purpose, you will realize that they are fundamental, and that this body of Christian men and women stands upon the fundamental principles of God's Word; that we have accepted the Holy Spirit as our Director; that we have pledged our loyalty to the interests and work of this great Fraternity, and that we are here to do business in the

Kingdom of God and for Him. I am praying that each one of us will realize all this, and that we shall come to the work of this meeting with a realization of our responsibility and our opportunity. We have a great work to do in the Kingdom of God. We have no small program before us. This is a meeting that demands your best thought, your purest emotion, and the best action which we can take today. I pray God that the Holy Spirit may lead us and direct us in all of our deliberations and actions of this hour.

After the rules of the meeting were read, he made the following remarks:

I have no remarks to make upon these rules. They are clear and I think you understand them. Most of you are acquainted with this, and yet I would like to explain so you will have no misunderstanding. There is only one way to get the floor to speak, and that is to address the Moderator and give your name. Both are necessary; the last especially necessary. You must give your name. I may know you but that makes no difference. We have our reporter who must know your name, so you will not be recognized until you have addressed the Moderator and have given your name. We shall endeavor to recognize that one whose name we first hear. It may save time to say just a few things concerning those who speak. As I have observed the work in former conventions, I have felt that there are two classes of people that need a little admonition. One does not have much to say but persists always in saying it, and the other does have something to say but refuses to say it. Now we are here to do business for the church. This is your business; it is not the business of the officers. We are here as your servants to help you. We want this work to move. If it moves, and if it goes as it should, you must do it. If you have a thought, if you have a speech, if you have a motion, if you have a question that will help us in the decision of this, you owe it to the conference to give it to us, but you do not have the right to take the time of this large delegate body to intrude upon them that which is irrelevant to the question at hand. I hope that during the deliberations of these hours every delegate will be thinking. A delegate who is not willing to think and to use these moments in thinking upon every question at hand has no right to be in the body. By your help and by observing these plain simple rules I am sure that the work of the Conference will move pleasantly. . . .

At the opening of his second year as moderator he spoke as follows:

If I understand the brethren of this body, it is that we now address ourselves to the business of this meeting, with as much haste as prudence may dictate. It is the work of the Standing Committee to prepare the business, that you may handle it as conveniently as possible. It gives me great pleasure to speak of the pleasant meetings the Standing Committee have held and the harmony which has existed in these meetings. The Standing Committee is made up of your representatives; they represent sections as widely apart and with as different customs as you yourselves represent; and yet our meetings have been very pleasant. If this General Conference can carry on its work as readily and harmoniously as the Standing Committee has done, we shall accomplish our work under the blessings of our Heavenly Father for the good of our great, beloved Brotherhood. . . . The church expects us to do our duty, and each of you should act under the inspiration of the broadened vision we have received during this Conference.[1]

At the close of the Conference he said:

I hardly see where or how any delegate can go home after listening to the splendid program we have had at this Conference, after listening to the splendid speeches that we have had the privilege of hearing, with a pessi-

[1] Excerpts from *Full Report of the Proceedings of the Annual Conference of the Church of the Brethren held at Calgary, Alberta, Canada, June 14 to 20, 1923.*

mistic report. Again I say that this Conference will stand out as one of the great events of our lives. May the Lord add His blessing to the work that has been done, and keep us faithful to Him and to His service. . . .[1]

WINGER ON THE FLOOR OF CONFERENCE

Perhaps no leader in his generation in the Church of the Brethren so well maintained the common touch as did Otho Winger. He himself came from the ranks of common people—farmers, laborers, small businessmen. He never ceased to enjoy association with them and found something to appreciate in them. He spoke their language, understood their struggles, knew their aspirations, and sympathized with them in their sorrows. He, better than most men, knew the religious convictions, the prejudices, and the aspirations of the rank and file of the common people. This knowledge he used to promote the causes in which he believed.

Furthermore, his courage and his manliness appealed to all classes. There was nothing weak, sentimental, or apologetic in him. He was fair, frank, courageous, and powerful for the right.

These qualities made him a force on the floor of Annual Conference. When one reads the full reports of the debates on the floor of that great assembly in the period from 1920 to 1935 one is impressed at the number of times, when an argument was on, that Otho Winger spoke for the majority, and not infrequently closed the argument, to the discomfiture of his opponents.

[1] *Ibid.*

It was always an amazing thing to realize how fully and quickly his mind comprehended the various implications of a given question. It was equally amazing how he could anticipate the possible objections before his opponents had opportunity to bring them up. His power on the floor of Conference often made him more influential when not a moderator than when he was presiding.

Four things gave him this power: (1) his judgment was usually sound; (2) he was by nature conservative and spoke the mind of the Conference-going church people; (3) people had confidence in him; and (4) he presented his cause in a self-confident, positive, and forceful manner.

His power of debate is shown in a discussion in Conference in 1922. A query had come to Conference asking for the appointment of a committee of "faithful, conservative Brethren not officially connected with a General Board, college or school of the Brotherhood to investigate the doctrinal position and doctrinal teachings of each of our schools and colleges, and to report to the conference of 1923."

At once Otho Winger asked for an explanation for this query being before the Conference. After the explanation was given he asked again whether complaints concerning any of the schools had come to the district sending the query. Being informed that some statements had been made by officials of some institutions which were not agreeable to many members of the Brotherhood, he then asked whether the district bringing the query had taken it up either with the schools or the General Educational Board. The reply being that such had not been done in either case, he then made the following speech on the floor. The address represents Otho Winger in his best parliamentary form:

I am not here to oppose an investigation of any institutions in the Church of the Brethren. I represent a college that belongs to the church, whose trustees, elected by the church, have a perfect right to investigate the work of the school, and the school at all times is open for visiting, for investigation. These trustees—I am speaking for our school, for I think our school represents somewhat the schools in the Brotherhood—are as faithful and competent as any to be found in the Brotherhood, and that is a part of the work they do each year, to investigate. This query evidently was prompted, as the answer of the delegate indicates, because reports were circulated and complaints made against certain teachings of the schools. I should like to have you notice also that the plaintiffs, before they brought it to this conference, neither went to the school nor to the General Educational Board. I leave it to you, fellow delegates, whether that proposition is right, whether that is even according to the ordinary rules of our Brotherhood. We have an Educational Board, and a part of its work, fundamentally assigned to it and so stated in the constitution, covers the point at issue, yet complaints are brought to the conference and aired before the membership, without ever having been presented to the General Educational Board. I would like to note what seems to me to be an unfair request concerning the committee. If this investigation were needed, the school men ought to be on. I would like to know why it is, when we have on our General Educational Board five—and some of the representatives on these Boards have no connection with any school or college—that these brethren, including some of the most faithful and some of the most talented, should be deprived of representation on this committee. I don't say that the District aimed at that, but some of us feel that this paper, coming without previous inquiry, is an insinuation and even an accusation, under cover, against every school in the Brotherhood.

I know you may say it isn't there, but suppose I were to arise in a business meeting and say to the chairman, "Let's investigate the honesty of John Smith." I haven't made any accusation. All I am doing is saying that we shall investigate the honesty of John Smith. Here we have a paper coming before this great Brotherhood, asking for a committee to investigate the doctrinal teachings. It doesn't say, of course, that the doctrinal teachings are not right, but it implies that. It suggests an accusation against the doctrinal teaching of the schools, and furthermore (I am not opposed to this from the general situation), there is a condition existing in our Brotherhood, in some places, that ought not to be so. I am with you on anything that will uphold the doctrines, the fundamental doctrines, of the Christian religion, but we have some things that are not for the best interests of our Brotherhood. I can illustrate by a personal example. It was my duty Sunday evening to preach in this Tabernacle. On Monday morning a good brother, whom I have known twenty years, said, "I was mighty glad that I heard you last night. I had been told that you do not believe in the Deity of Jesus Christ, and I am glad I heard that sermon." Some people thought I had fixed it up for a defense for this particular occasion. One brother said, "I have heard you preach that sermon six times." I have been preaching it for the last twenty years. I am giving you this to show something that is happening throughout the Brotherhood. Not long ago a sister in the church said to one of our people, "Do you know that such and such an elder does not believe in the Deity of Jesus Christ, and yet that elder has been appointed on one of the most important committees." That ought not to be. There are people, with assumed piety, who will whisper that this brother, that brother, this school, that school, is not standing to the fundamentals, and that thing, I know, has injured some people. In the business

123

world you could circulate statements that would affect my business, and I would have recourse, but somehow we have an opportunity in the church to whisper about a church member, a minister, possibly an institution, most any sort of thing, and it passes. If there is anything we ought to guard it is the principles of our church. If an individual in a school is not standing for them, there ought to be an investigation. A man who does not believe in the Deity of Jesus Christ ought not to be in the church. He confessed to that belief, and it is a most serious thing in our church to deny that which is sealed with the most sacred ordinance. If this is a serious thing, it is also serious to accuse a man. It is a serious thing to be guilty of a crime, but it is almost as serious to accuse a man. This last, I grant, is not implied in this paper. But it explains the general situation, which ought not to exist in our Brotherhood. I represent a school that does not fear an investigation. I don't care how many committees you send. If things aren't what they ought to be, they should be investigated. I am opposed to a paper that comes from a District, from people who have a complaint, who have never gone to the schools with it, and have never approached our Educational Board, to which our General Conference has given just such matters to investigate. I feel, with all seriousness, and with all due regard to the brethren that brought this paper— though their purpose is good, according to the purity of the church—that it ought to be sent back.[1]

After considerable discussion the paper was respectfully returned. This settled an important issue and school men long remembered the contributions President Winger made to its settlement.

For a long time there was considerable dissention in the church growing out of differences of practice in the enforcement of church requirements

---

[1] *Full Report of the Proceedings of the Annual Conference of the Church of the Brethren Held at Winona Lake, Indiana, June 7 to 15, 1922.* Pages 181, 182.

regarding dress and other matters. Liberal churches would grant letters of membership to people moving into conservative churches and thus make it difficult for conservative churches to keep up their requirements. Conservative churches often refused to grant letters to members who would not conform to their technical requirements. Some would simply delay action or refuse to take action. A query was before the 1924 Conference recommending that churches be forced to take some action, either to grant letters or to grant them with exceptions noted on the back of the certificates. Otho Winger's speech on this question follows:

I think a motion to pass a paper of this kind does not prevent a discussion of any part of it; and there is no disposition on the part of anybody to shut off any discussion. I like the report for two or three reasons. In one respect, I do not see that it shuts off any church from doing what it has done in the past. If it is the dress question, if it's the lodge question, if it's any other question, and you do not want your members to do that thing, and you do not think that a man is worthy of membership who does it, you have a right to attend to it. And what's more, you have a duty to attend to it. Now, this does one thing that ought to be done in our church. We have had a lot of churches in the past from which members have moved, and the members cannot get letters, but the churches don't do anything about it. All they do is not to grant the letter. I would like to see something that would move a church up. The reason they don't give letters is because they don't have—should I say—the boldness to take a stand on the proposition. They just simply won't grant the letter. And that's where the thing stands. I think we ought to have something on our Minutes that would require a church to act, and if a member is in a church, to whom they will not give a letter, they either ought to reach that matter, or be compelled to turn the member over so somebody else could. There isn't anything in this report that prevents a church from disciplining its members. And I have a conviction that if a brother or a sister is carried on church membership, if he's worthy to be carried at all, there should be some provision by which, when he moves to another locality, he should be transferred there. There are two reasons why I am in favor of this. I think the reasoning and the interpretation are entirely wrong. There is nothing in this to prevent a church from disciplining its members. If it's a question of dress, or a question of lodge, the church has the same right to do a thing that I think should be done. A church does not have the right to withhold a letter for years, without taking a stand on the question. Let them turn the matter over to the larger church; if it does not want to accept it; that's their privilege. But I do believe it will remedy what I consider to be a serious wrong in our method of church government just now.[1]

In 1918, at a time when there was still much opposition to the use of pianos in many churches, the piano issue came to Annual Conference. Otho Winger made the following speech on that subject:

I thought a while ago we were ready to vote on the question. It is very easy, I know, to say, after hearing a twelve-minute speech, that there was nothing in it. I am not going to say that about anything that has been said here, but it did seem to me that we had heard sufficient to bring us to the close of the argument on this question. I am in favor of the answer of the Standing Committee. I am not going to repeat the reasons for it. I am not in favor of bringing the musical instrument into use in our services. I am not opposed to it on the ground that it is morally wrong. I have a musical instru-

<hr />

[1] *Full Report of the Proceedings of the Annual Conference of the Church of the Brethren held at Hershey, Pennsylvania, June 4 to 11, 1924.* Pages 85, 86.

ment in my home which the boys use. I can handle that matter to suit myself. We can vary its use as we please. I am opposed to this on the ground of practicability. There are two things that stand out in my mind on this question. If you have musical instruments in general use in your church, there are two things that prevail. One is there is less effort—as has been said to you this morning—on the part of those who sing, and more dependence upon the instrument. In the second place, there is in every congregation only perhaps a minority—at least not by any means a large part of the congregation —that is used to singing by the instrument, and it is an observation that those people are not at home and don't feel at home so readily when the instrument is used. Now, I happen to have a little experience with young people. Young people can do and will do most anything and follow most any sort of an ideal that you set up before them. If you give them the idea that they cannot sing without a musical instrument, they have that idea, and if you give them the idea that they are able of themselves to sing with the spirit and with the understanding, they can do that, too. We have young people in our school, and about as many as they have in other places in the Brotherhood, and we have not used a musical instrument in the Chapel for seven years. We don't want it in. One man, who had visited ten colleges, many of which had used instruments, said that the singing in our Chapel was the climax of anything he had heard. Now, another thing about it, some felt a little bit alarmed when our class in music wanted to give the oratorio, "Daniel," and their argument was that you cannot do it without musical instruments, and the answer we gave was, "You cannot do it unless you can without musical instruments." They went into the work with a zeal and an interest that they would not have exhibited had they the aid of the musical instruments, and they did it. Now, we know it can be done. I know the argument has been brought up this morning that where the numbers are few you need an instrument. Well, I don't know about that. It doesn't take a large number of people to sing if you sing with spirit and understanding. Generally, out in these places or where they are so few, they don't notice even if one or two are out of tune. I might argue all day, and then you might say there has been no argument given on this question. I won't argue the question any more, but there is one practical reason that I want to leave with you as to why we ought to adopt the answer of Standing Committee. You can pass this question if you want to, and you can say it is to be done only when there is no objection, but you know, and this delegate body knows, what this would project upon our churches, at a time when we ought to bend every energy we have and every effort we have and every thought we have towards the church needs that are before us. You know as well as I know the result it would have upon the Brotherhood, and especially at a time when we ought to bend every thought to the big questions before us, and we ought to close this discussion and spend our time on things that are of more vital importance. We ought not to inject anything into this Brotherhood that would divide us, but rather we should go forward united on the great issues that are in the church today, and I am in favor of the answer of Standing Committee, and I hope it will pass.

It was because of his conservative stand on some questions such as the piano that some Brethren in more remote areas of the church considered him a reactionary and formed a wrong impression of him. As a result they underestimated his real strength and influence.

In a letter to H. C. Early written in 1933, Otho Winger said he regarded his "writing of the substitute motion at the Lincoln Conference in 1926 about the best service I have ever done for the church." The background of the statement is this: For a number of years gradual changes had been taking place in the church. A transition was on in the whole social life of America and naturally it affected the church, especially in urban centers. The church had stressed the simple life in dress and had adopted forms for both men and women as a means of attaining it. Women were to wear a veil in worship in fulfillment of Paul's injunction in First Corinthians 11. The church had also endorsed a Quaker bonnet as approved headgear for women, and a standing-collar coat for men. The church was opposed to secret orders and no one who was a member of a secret order was to be admitted to the church. The wearing of jewelry was forbidden and bobbed hair was obnoxious to the church. Kneeling in prayer was the custom and the salutation of the holy kiss was observed. Musical instruments were not used in the church, but congregational singing without instruments was generally practiced.

In many places these formal restrictions were breaking down. Some churches ceased enforcing the form of dress. In certain churches it was reported that ministers and elders received into the church people who were members of secret societies. The piano was introduced into some churches. Others no longer knelt in prayer. Then, too, there were evidences of the increasing use of jewelry. Some women began to bob their hair and were accused of "wearing apparel in quality and style that borders on indecency and shamelessness."

Some of the older members of the church were disturbed by these manifestations of "worldliness." In a church that had always stressed simplicity of life and separation from the world, these matters seemed evidences of spiritual decline and a departure from the faith. This was particularly true in certain areas, especially in Pennsylvania and certain other sections where they still adhered rigidly to the form of dress.

One cannot seriously question the sincerity of many of these. It is, however, also easy for those who seem to love controversy to become leaders of factions and take advantage of such a situation.

Many who were disturbed by these irregularities wrote bitter articles for the *Gospel Messenger*, which was the official church paper. Some of these articles were printed, but naturally the *Gospel Messenger* could not be a constant forum of controversy for the discussion of these issues—especially in a time when other important, forward-looking issues faced the church.

As a result some of the leaders of discontent started a church paper of their own called the *Monitor*, in which they aired their views, made attacks on the "worldliness" in the church, and caustically attacked the *Gospel Messenger*, the church boards, and the church institutions such as the colleges.

This discontent was never wholly absent in the church. It was considerably strengthened at about the close of World War I and rose to great heights in the early twenties.

It was, then, in the twenties, especially in 1923, 1924, 1925, and 1926, that Otho Winger made herculean efforts to deal with the discontented elements and to prevent a split in the church. He had correspondence with most of those who were writing for the *Monitor*. Of this we shall speak in another connection. In this correspondence he showed himself at his greatest strength. He considered himself a conservative and generally *Monitor* leaders also so considered him. He always wore the plain attire of the Brethren. He was on the side of the simple life; he loved the humble people of the church. He knew the sorrow and heartaches caused by the split in the church in 1881 and 1882 and he wanted to prevent another. A review of his correspondence shows that he waged a one-man campaign in an attempt to hold as many as he could loyal to the church. He wrote scores of letters, many of them two-, three-, and four-page single-spaced letters, pleading for unity and cooperation.

One of the centers of conservative sentiment in the church was in the districts of Eastern Pennsylvania and Southern Pennsylvania. These people lived in the area of the earliest centers of Brethren life. President Winger had high regard for them. He believed them to be sincere and devout. They gave generously to the cause of missions and to the general program of the church. Their lives seemed to reflect the sincerity of their convictions. Here was pure, primitive "Dunkerism." He had great respect for their leaders. He distinguished their conservatism from that of some who had never accomplished much for the church and who seemed bent on agitation and on splitting the church. They were a group not identified with the *Monitor* and its allied movement.

In 1926 at the Annual Conference held at Lincoln, Nebraska, matters came to a head. Otho Winger believed that the leaders who were promoting the *Monitor* movement were ready to break with the church and start an independent movement. In fact, he told them so. At the same time Eastern Pennsylvania and Southern Pennsylvania had almost identical queries at the Conference asking that no one be sent or retained as a missionary who is unsound in fundamentals or who will not comply with Conference rulings on the dress question; that no elder who receives a member into the church belonging to a secret society should be allowed to sit in District or Annual Conference. Elders were admonished to be faithful in teaching and enforcing the simple life and in not allowing bobbed hair; officials were to encourage the family altar and see that sisters wear the prayer veil, and observe the salutation of the holy kiss.

This was the problem that now confronted Otho Winger. The leaders from Eastern Pennsylvania wanted many of the same things for which the *Monitor* was contending. If they were not satisfied at the Lincoln Conference some fourteen thousand of the finest Brethren from Pennsylvania might join the movement that was ready to break with the church. He believed that the real leaders of Pennsylvania wanted to stay with the church if they could be satisfied, but that the recalcitrant leaders of the *Monitor* movement would do all they could to get the Eastern and Southern Pennsylvania Brethren to go with them.

In his own words he says that the papers from

Pennsylvania could not pass. They were "rigid, harsh, reactionary." They "could have started a lot of trouble. We could not discuss the matter in Standing Committee because the papers had an answer." Everybody wondered what would happen.[1] In a letter to H. C. Early, seven years later, he wrote,

On Monday night before the Conference was to begin on Tuesday, I began to think seriously. To have those papers come before Annual Conference and be turned down would have been an insult to eastern and southern Pennsylvania. I was afraid some harsh things would be said. To have that happen with this other organization at hand might have resulted seriously. I spent most of Monday night in my hotel trying to write out a substitute answer to that paper. I wrote it again and again. The papers were long. I tried to cover the points in the paper, restating the principles of the church in them, but leaving out the teeth and the reactionary part of it.

The following is the resolution he produced and presented to the Conference the next day:

Realizing that in many ways the members of our beloved church are prone to drift into worldly thought and conduct, and sincerely desiring to do all possible to keep our church true to the teachings of our Lord and His work, therefore the Annual Meeting of 1926 reaffirms some of her fundamental teachings and urges renewed faithfulness to them.

1. That all our ministers and missionaries be true to the declaration of principles and purpose as required of all delegates to Annual Meeting.

2. That we continue our opposition to our members

---

[1] If a district puts an answer to a query from a church, Standing Committee must pass it on to Conference without change. If no answer comes from the district then Standing Committee may form an answer and submit it to open Conference.

belonging to secret societies and oath bound organizations and insist that pastors and elders do not receive into or hold in church membership those who are members of such organizations.

3. That elders and pastors be faithful in teaching the simple life; that our members refrain from wearing immodest dress and jewelry and from worldly amusements. We decide that the worldly custom of women bobbing their hair is contrary to scripture and Christian modesty and urge all our sisters to adorn themselves as women professing godliness.

4. That all our members make a united effort to have the family altar erected in every home; that worship in our churches be made as spiritual as possible; and that the Lord's prayer and the kneeling posture be not neglected.

5. That we renew our vows of love for the Church of the Brethren and for one another and urge that the Christian salutation of the Holy Kiss, that great symbol of Christian love, be properly observed.

To continue in the words of his letter to H. C. Early:

Next morning I went down to the grounds. I saw I. W. Taylor. I said to him, "Brother Taylor, your paper from eastern Pennsylvania can't pass. What would you think of this as an answer?" He read it once. He read it twice. I shall never forget when he looked up at me and said, "If our paper can't pass, this will satisfy eastern Pennsylvania." I went to Charley Baker. He was happy for it. I didn't get to see many before the business meeting. The papers came up early. Without much discussion I introduced my substitute. It was warmly seconded. Not a man from Pennsylvania opposed it. Kessler and his group did, but the substitute passed. Eastern and southern Pennsylvania were satisfied. The leaders went home happy but a crisis had been passed and Brethren Hertzler, Taylor and Longenecker did a lasting good . . . by urging their members not to go with the new movement.

The new movement (the Dunkard Brethren movement) did not amount to much, "but should those men have chosen to join it, the church would have had a bigger divide than that of 1881. Since that time our danger is past. Since that time we have been free to talk fraternal relations." This was Otho Winger's statement made in 1933, describing what had happened at Lincoln in 1926.

As evidence of the effectiveness of his work at the 1926 Conference is this letter sent some time early in the summer of 1926 by Elders I. W. Taylor, J. H. Longenecker, and Samuel H. Hertzler, three of the stalwarts of eastern Pennsylvania and members of the district ministerial board, to the ministers and other disaffected people of their district.

Dear Brother ———,

According to what we regard as reliable information, the thing that some of us have for some time been fearing, and which it seems to us none would really want, has happened, or is at the point of happening.

We are told that a group of our dear brethren and sisters have about decided to withdraw their fellowship from the Church of the Brethren with a view of forming another and separate organization. We would indeed deeply deplore a step of this kind. It would bring back again as from the grave all the dark record, the painful experiences, and horrors of things that happened some forty years ago, which in large measure are forgotten by the present generation.

Experience has taught us that division was no cure then. We have no reason to believe it will mean a cure now. Above all there is no assurance that it would meet the approval of the Father of mercies. Isa. 54:7-10, Jer. 31:35-37, Cor. 12:25. Scripture has no plain case where God countenances division.

The story of Elijah and the record of the seven churches of Asia, Rev. 2 and 3, cannot be reconciled with the idea of forsaking the church or of bringing about a rupture in the church. Some of us who felt there was just cause for complaint were greatly encouraged at our last Annual Conference by the attitude of our church leaders. We therefore think it would indeed be very unfortunate to agitate or disturb the church with a spirit of division at a time when there is hope of a check to the worldly trend in the main body of the church.

While we are not unmindful of the many problems with which the faithful are confronted in these last days, and the trials and tests it brings to them, we, however, do not think that our people in eastern Pennsylvania would be ready for another break in the Brotherhood.

We take this opportunity, which may seem to be a late date to earnestly plead with our dear brethren and sisters, to be cautious and move slow in an issue fraught with such grave and tremendous responsibilities.

Ministerial Board of Eastern Pennsylvania:

I. W. Taylor
J. H. Longenecker
Samuel H. Hertzler

The above story has been related in detail and some of it in President Winger's own words to show his method of work, his hold on the conservative leaders of the church, and his concern to hold the church together. The fact that he related this story in a letter more than seven years later to H. C. Early is an indication of his estimate of the significance of the Lincoln Conference. In fact, in the letter he says, "As I see it, that was the most serious conference that I ever attended."

In his early days President Winger had several times opposed the appointment of a Fraternal Relations Committee to attempt a reunion with the

Progressive wing of the church and thus heal the break of 1882. In this letter to H. C. Early in 1933, he explains his reason for this opposition. He felt that now an approach to the Progressive Brethren could be made without fear of the loss of the conservative wing of the church. Before this an effort to join with the Progressives would have resulted in losing the conservatives, he thought.

HIS INFLUENCE THROUGH CORRESPONDENCE

Otho Winger was a great letter writer. Those of us who worked near him know that for many years he retired after midnight and sometimes at one or two o'clock more often than before midnight. He had an old Oliver typewriter. He had learned the "hunt and peck" system. For a long time he seemed to punch the keys with one finger of each hand. Later he developed greater skill and speed. There were often erasures and sections were sometimes crossed out, but his message came through just the same. Who of us who knew him do not cherish some of these letters?

The range of his correspondence was enormous. He spent hours and hours writing letters everywhere on all sorts of matters. And his letters were not short, cryptic ones such as some of us write who have difficulty with our typing. Many of his letters were two and three pages long, single-spaced, pounded out in the late hours of the night or the "wee hours" of the morning. Once his diary records, "Wrote twenty-five letters at night," and another time, "Wrote letters till 2 a.m."

The list of his correspondents includes practically all those in the responsible positions of the Church of the Brethren of his day. A roster of names in the files, to most of whom he wrote a number of letters that have come to the writer's hand, includes the names of the following churchmen: Enoch Eby, D. L. Miller, I. B. Trout, Galen Royer, H. C. Early, J. H. Moore, J. J. Yoder, I. W. Taylor, J. H. Longenecker, J. H. B. Williams, C. C. Ellis, Paul Bowman, A. C. Wieand, D. W. Kurtz, B. E. Kessler, A. P. Blough, Charles D. Bonsack, Ezra Flory, Grant Mahan, Edward Frantz, Robert Arnold, I. J. Rosenberger, S. S. Blough, Manly Deeter, Frank Fisher, D. M. Garver, J. F. Hoke, David Hollinger, J. W. Lear, J. K. Miller, Levi Minnich, Jacob Coppock, George L. Studebaker, Jesse Stutsman, L. W. Teeter, J. Edson Ulrey, G. A. Snyder, E. S. Young, and W. H. Yoder.

In addition there are many letters to missionaries in the fields, members of boards, board secretaries, and many laymen from various parts of the country.

It is amazing, however, to note how many other people wrote to President Winger from various parts of the United States to get advice and help on difficult church problems. Collected in one file marked "Church Letters, General," were found letters covering the years 1924-1934, from the following addresses: Modesto, California; Pyrmont, Indiana; Elizabethtown, Pennsylvania; Waverly, Kansas; Arcadia, Indiana; Woodbury, Pennsylvania; Mabel, Oregon; Goshen, Indiana; Alvordton, Ohio; Logansport, Indiana; Thomas, Oklahoma; Pioneer, Ohio;

Virden, Illinois; St. Joseph, Missouri; Johnstown, Pennsylvania; Goshen, Indiana; Canfield, Ohio; Pittsburgh, Pennsylvania; Eaton, Ohio; Berne, Indiana; Harrisburg, Pennsylvania; Troy, Ohio; Nevada, Iowa; Omak, Washington; Middlebury, Indiana; Bradford, Ohio; Nampa, Idaho; Garrett, Indiana; Cando, North Dakota; Hagerstown, Maryland; Elgin, Illinois; and Elkhart, Indiana.

It is to be noted that these were personal letters written to Otho Winger for advice. Some correspondents wrote for interpretation of the rules of the church regarding divorce or what to do in cases of divorced people. Some were asking for personal advice. Others were asking, as elders of churches, what to do in cases of divorced people. This question came up in several varieties. In one community the report had circulated that the chairman of the General Mission Board received a larger salary than the president of the United States. The pastor of the church wrote to get the facts. He got them "hot" from the pen of Otho Winger though the pastor himself was blameless. Some asked whether sisters could serve as delegates. Some raised questions about the use of a piano in the church or where to try a certain minister guilty of misconduct. Some asked about the use of books that are unorthodox. Some desired opening the pages of the *Gospel Messenger* for more debate. A mother with a disobedient child wrote for help. Questions about war and an attitude toward it were raised. Some asked what to do with a Sunday-school superintendent who had bobbed hair and wore immodest dress. One asked about preaching the second coming of Christ.

A great many wanted to know what to do about all the worldliness creeping into the church. Others asked regarding church government and church discipline.

To these letters he gave careful reply. Occasionally his replies were fiery and vehement, especially to captious, quarrelsome writers. Many times he went into a scrupulous, thoughtful discussion of the questions asked and gave good, wholesome, common-sense advice. He was courageous and diplomatic. But he would not allow himself to be drawn into local controversies or pronounce judgment on an issue when he was not near enough to review the case thoroughly.

One can well ask why there were so many letters to him from throughout the Brotherhood. The answer is that he had been moderator of Conference many times. His speeches at Annual Conference and his articles in the *Gospel Messenger* identified him with the traditional position of the church. He was chairman of the Mission Board. He had helped revise the minutes of the Annual Conference and knew the rules of the church. All these things increased the confidence of the loyal, conservative people of the church in the soundness of the advice he gave.

It is amazing to see the volume of correspondence which poured from his desk on a cause that seemed urgent. There were several crucial issues during his life concerning which he wrote letters which, if printed and bound, would make a good-sized volume. This was especially true regarding the *Monitor* movement and the threat of the division of the church at that time, and regarding some issues in the China and Africa mission fields. The writer read hundreds of these letters and has been forced to conclude that the measure of President Winger's influence was enormously increased throughout the church by these epistles full of enthusiasm, of sound advice, of optimism and moral courage. A man who writes letters by the scores daily from twenty to thirty years cannot fail to touch the lives of many, many people whom he would otherwise but slightly influence.

In no situation did he so assiduously and relentlessly apply his correspondence as he did in connection with the *Monitor* movement, which led to the withdrawal of the Dunkard Brethren from the main body of the church. For the years 1923, 1924, 1925, 1926, he carried on an effective campaign of letter writing with those who were connected with the Dunkard Brethren movement. Some not at all connected with that movement wrote him for counsel and advice. Some may have written to protest in the hope that he could help. To those who wrote articles for the *Monitor* he wrote most vigorously, trying to dissuade them from their bitter attacks on the church. He felt sure that such attacks would lead to further division, which he dreaded.

These discontented people felt that Otho Winger was one of the leaders of the church who had the most sympathy for their cause, one whom they could approach in confidence. Such expressions as the following are found in letters directed to him:

I had the highest regard for you.
I write to you because I feel that you have a powerful

influence as to the policies of the church and the colleges.

Is there another Elder in the Brotherhood that has as much influence in A. M. [Annual Meeting] to work out something that would do this very thing as Otho Winger?

I am sure that you see what the tendency has been and I have believed that you are not in favor of the church losing her identity as a non-worldly body.

I had intended to make some sort of an appeal to you to see whether you would not use all the influence you have to check the steady and accelerating march of the church toward the world.

The following paragraphs are from letters received by him from those disturbed by the worldly tendencies in the church.

Are we to let things drift or are we to try to stem the tide? Are we to be ruled by the secret society men? Is the wearing of gold to be allowed to go on? Are we to become as fashionable as other denominations? Are we to become as lax in discipline as they are? The command is to come out and be separate. Are we going to heed it?

I am confident you would like to see the church be true to herself and to her Lord. You know and I know she is not being true, and that conditions are getting worse and not better. Our members are more given over to pride and fashion, to lodges, to worldliness than ever before. Our elders are not standing for what we profess to believe. We have congregations in which pride and fashion have come in by way of the elders' families—and the members seem to love it. . . . All the power of the church has been in his [the elder's] hands for years. . . . We are no longer allowed to elect a man to the ministry without having outside elders come in and tell us what man to vote for. In our elections the Holy Spirit has been ruled out.

Later letters complain that the pages of the *Gospel Messenger* are no longer open to the Brethren who would protest against the evils coming into the church. As a result the new paper, the *Monitor*, was started by B. E. Kessler and his friends as the vehicle of discontent.

To these correspondents, Otho Winger replied in single-spaced typewritten letters, two or three pages in length, written in haste, with vigor, and at times it seems with vehemence. There is no effort at literary excellence. His messages go directly to the point and are evidently written with the sincere desire to dissuade the detractors of the church and to prevent another unfortunate division.

To those who found too much worldliness in the church he could honestly reply as follows:

First, as to the movement, I can sympathize with any member who is not satisfied with the worldliness in the world and in the church. I would welcome any movement that would lessen that. But I have never known of a time when there was not much of that. I read Paul's letters to Corinth; he had about as much as we had to deal with. Some of the Monitor writers talk of the good old days of the Church before 1911. But I happen to know of some of the ugliness before then too. If another divide in our church would help that, it would do good, but seriously I doubt it.

Now you say you are going to fight worldliness. God bless you, if you go in God's name. But there are some of us who have been fighting the devil about as long as you and still are. . . . I say again, Brother ———, if you are fighting worldliness and upholding the Gospel teaching, I am with you. . . . I think I need say [no] more. Wherein you are striving for the best things in life for the church and the work of the Lord, I am with you. I am as interested in the Peace question as anyone. I welcome and urge anything we can get on that subject in the "Messenger," or any other church doctrine. I shall be with any one who works in a constructive way, even if we do not agree always, but I shall be most vigorously against much that is being written and done by the Monitor circle.

To dissuade those who would divide the church he argued: "I hesitate to think of what it will mean in ugly feelings, families torn asunder, neighborhoods upset, contests over church property, etc. Most of the older people I have talked to who lived through that and where that occurred dread to see the like again."

To those who wanted to go back to the good old days, he queried to what good old days they would go back and pointed out that if they went back far enough to the really old decisions none of the malcontents could now be members. He pointed out that a church organized on the plan advocated by these discontented people would have to give up foreign missions, school work, city missions, and much other work, for young people would be put out or kept out of the church.

And while most are now united in their criticism of the church, it will only need time until you will be criticizing each other as much as you now do the church.

As much as I would like to have things different in the church, I cannot wish the present movement any success. And if the predicted divide comes, I shall find myself obliged to do all I can to keep the church intact and keep it from the influence of those who would lead many out of the church that I love.

I should rather hope that better councils will prevail and that those who have such love for the right will remain with the church and endeavor to direct the work and lives of our people in the way that they should go. We need all of that we can get and I shall welcome it.

But we do not need any further division, which in my estimation will be a sin and a tragedy on the part of those concerned.

For a more vigorous direct appeal to one who supported the *Monitor* movement, the following letter, which shows the force, the directness, and the dead earnestness of Otho Winger, is one of the best:

I have read the Monitor from start till now. Again and again there are articles that lampoon the work of the church, the annual meeting, the boards appointed by annual meeting, the mission work, the educational work, in fact most everything. I need not quote. I can when necessary. As long as that was the work of one man that mattered little. I thought of it as the last standing committee expressed itself, that it was hardly worth noticing. But when a group of men, most of whom have written the schismatic articles, meet on the way to conference, to organize a paper contrary to the decision of conference, and after their triumphal work come on to conference and enter into the work of that conference which they have condemned in the paper they are upholding, when that happens then it is time to call a halt. And I predict that will happen before another year.

You say the Monitor does not want division. No, but it wants its own way. It wants to say its say, anything about the conference and her workers and still be considered loyal. There has been much said in the Monitor about loyalty to Annual Meeting. But never in my acquaintance have I known any group of men who have violated so many decisions of Annual Meeting. . . . Your publication of it is direct contradiction to the work of the conference. Let alone the railing against decision after decision of the conference. No there will be no trouble with a lot of folks if they can have their own way and say their own say, but when that procedure strikes at the very heart of the church and her unity, it is time to consider.

Now your explanations sound good and your articles sound good, but brother ———, the one thing you are doing, you are upholding the Monitor and making it possible. And there is where you and I differ most sharply. I am opposed to the Monitor, to its policy, to its spirit and to the type of men who are upholding it. Whatever is good, and there has been some good, it can be gotten through the Messenger, and scattered a hundred times as far. You say you do not want a radical sheet like the Vindicator. I read both papers and I tell you the Vindicator is liberal in its tone and Christian in its spirit compared to the Monitor, as it has been.

And I want to say to you, my brother, and say it as kindly as I ever said anything to any one, and frank as I ever said anything, and I have to say frank things to a lot of folks, that IF THE MONITOR GOES ON, WITH ITS MOST CERTAIN RESULTS, YOU ARE MORE RESPONSIBLE RIGHT NOW THAN ANY OTHER MAN, unless it be ———. And I would have you consider brother, the use you are making of the Lord's money, and the responsibility you must carry for the results. You say you are opposed to division, but the Monitor family as a whole is not, many of them talking it and are blocking the work of the church wherever they can because they expect division. And the Monitor cannot go on without division. For if the Church of the Brethren has gone to the world, as the Monitor writers say it has, but which I do not believe, there is no use for the Monitor to attempt to bring it back to the Monitor's point of view. I know the church in this section and I know that the Monitor will be powerless in its present message and spirit. For the Church of the Brethren will never retrace her steps on Missions, Education, salaried ministry, women preaching, ministerial boards, the instruments in churches, nor will she turn out every one who does not wear the bonnet as ——— would have it done. I have often been wrong, and may be here, but you are facing a hopeless task if you uphold the Monitor and try to carry out her teachings.

Otho Winger as a Churchman

I suppose I have already done the foolish thing . . . writing two pages, when I might have begun right here to say what I really wanted to say. If you are sincere in your desire to have the Gospel Messenger to be more open to Gospel articles, and would at all care to meet with the directors of the Publishing House, I think I can assure you of a welcome to the next meeting. You can present to the board and the editor your complaints as well as your suggestions about the Messenger. This is only my personal expression for the present, but I feel sure other members of the board would join in also.

This represents Otho Winger at his greatest force, though perhaps not in his greatest effectiveness. When one realizes that this man who was at the heart of the church organization and one of its most effective leaders was writing to most of the leaders of the opposition, one gets some idea of the strategic position he held. Strangely, many of his predictions have come true, and when those who left the church were ready to come back Otho Winger was most kindly in making it easy to have them return.

His Work for Missions

Otho Winger was elected to the General Mission Board of the church in 1912 to succeed L. W. Teeter and for thirty years his name was intimately associated with that of missions in the Church of the Brethren. For sixteen of those years he was chairman of the board. He was thirty-five years of age when first appointed to membership on the board.

One is not certain why he was chosen for this task. He probably had had a long-time interest in missions. He and his wife had been members of Our Missionary Reading Circle. During a few past Annual Conferences he had occasionally made a speech and had evidently impressed the leadership of the church. He had also been doing some writing in the *Gospel Messenger*. He had a growing reputation as a preacher and teacher and had in the previous year been elected president of Manchester College, factors which called his name to the attention of the Brotherhood.

When he began service on the board it consisted of the following members: H. C. Early, Galen B. Royer, J. J. Yoder, C. D. Bonsack, and himself, with D. L. Miller as life advisory member and J. H. B. Williams as secretary. The chairman was then H. C. Early. Otho Winger was a great admirer of H. C. Early and said of him: "He was a great general and leader of men. Four years with him on the General Educational Board and twelve years on the General Mission Board together with many other services on various committees brought to me much valuable training in church work." And in the letter to Early he wrote: "I think of you as a father and one of the greatest teachers." Galen B. Royer had been secretary of the board for some years and was now a member. His wide experience and long service made his presence there valuable.

J. J. Yoder from Kansas, then in his early forties, who was on the board through nearly all of President Winger's period of service, was one of the strong members of the board, and for him Otho Winger had great affinity and strong admiration. When they agreed, things happened. When they differed, which they sometimes did, a strong debate followed, and often nothing happened. In 1940, he wrote to Yoder saying, "I want to tell you again that I have never worked with a man in our church for whom I had greater esteem than I have for you."

Charles D. Bonsack of Maryland, also in his forties, was a member of the board at this time and later was its secretary. For many, many years there flowed between him and Otho Winger a constant stream of correspondence which if gathered together would make several volumes of interesting reading and would constitute a history of the missions of the church for that period, and incidentally reveal much about the two men. The two men were very different, but each admired the other and expressed his appreciation for the other. The letters of Charles D. Bonsack during these years show him to have been one of the most gracious, considerate, kindly, and cultured men in the life of the church.

It is not clear how much contact D. L. Miller had with the board during these years. He was seventy-one years of age when Otho Winger was appointed to it, and died in 1921, nine years later. Of him Brother Winger said, "He was a great soul and a great church father. His rich experience in years of travel made association with him very valuable." And, in turn, already in 1916 D. L. Miller wrote to Otho Winger saying, "I thank God for your useful, helpful life in the great work of the Church. On the Mission Board, in the educational work, you are doing so well. God bless you and give you many, many years of your useful service."

J. H. B. Williams was then secretary of the board and there are extant some beautiful and gracious letters between these two strong young men. Others of his associates on the board during his active period were A. P. Blough of Waterloo, Iowa, J. B. Emmert, Levi Garst, H. H. Nye, Frank Carper, B. F. Studebaker, W. Newton Long, Leland Brubaker, and Rufus D. Bowman. Other staff people who sustained various relationships to him during this period were H. Spenser Minnich, assistant secretary; M. R. Zigler, home missions secretary; C. M. Culp, treasurer; and Leland Brubaker, secretary following C. D. Bonsack. With all these he kept up a sustained correspondence. For him they maintained a profound respect, as is revealed in their letters.

Those who worked near President Winger at the college were not highly aware of the great amount of energy he was giving to missions. When it came time for board meetings he would work all day in his office at the college, go to Warsaw by car, a distance of twenty miles, and either take a night train or an early morning train and be at Elgin for work in the morning. There he would work morning, afternoon, and evening for one, two, or three days, sometimes longer, take a late evening train, and be back for work at the college in the morning. This was not an occasional, but his usual, schedule. His hundreds of letters for missions were written at night.

While he discussed some of the problems of missions with his college associates, usually he said comparatively little about them except when some of our alumni were sent to the field.

He influenced missions through several means, the first being, of course, through the board itself. Before becoming chairman he showed himself to be a man of conviction, of good judgment, and of courage. He was aggressive and venturesome on matters in which he had faith. Being rapid in his mental processes, sound in his judgment, and clear in his convictions, as well as courageous, he soon exercised great leadership. Other men followed him. They selected him as chairman when he was the youngest member of the board. They held him in that position for more than sixteen years. Letters from missionaries in the field indicated that they had great confidence in his judgment and in his sense of fairness. They knew, too, that he was sincerely interested in missions, and in them personally.

As chairman of the board, he often presided at the missionary convocation at Annual Conference and at the commissioning of missionaries. This brought him before the leaders of the church as the representative of the missionary cause and its spokesman, this, too, at a time when the missionary movement was riding the crest of the wave of interest among Protestant groups in America. It was the era of John R. Mott, Robert E. Speer, Sherwood Eddy, and Robert Wilder. It was the era of the Student Volunteer conventions with their slogan, "Christianize the world in this generation." All this national interest in missions enhanced the movement in the church and gave power as well as support to the Mission Board.

It is also of some importance, as was indicated earlier, that the Mission Board in the Church of the

Brethren was one of the oldest boards of the church, that it had the benefit of the influence of some of the best leaders of the church in its earliest days, and that it was the only board of the church which had much money. The Sunday School Board, the Ministerial Board, and the Welfare Board each had a mere pittance as compared to the Mission Board. It had power because it had money! Then, too, the Mission Board members were also ex-officio directors of the Brethren Publishing House. This gave them the means for promoting their program as vigorously as they chose.

It is a compliment to the members of the Board that in 1935 they decided that they would guarantee to every other board in the church its needed budget out of the total giving of the church and then operate their own program from the remainder. Otho Winger had an important share in bringing about this arrangement.

He did much preaching on missions as the "great first-work of the church." In his sermon outlines we find topics like the following: *Jesus Christ and the Church in Missions; The Supreme Duty of the Church; The Local Congregation and Missions; Missions; Acts 1:8; The Great Commission; The Mission of the Apostolic Church;* and *The Mission of Life.*

On these occasions he spoke with great conviction and great enthusiasm. His argument was that missions was to be the chief work of the church, that the command of Jesus was to go, that the early spread of the gospel was through missionaries, such as Paul and Barnabas, who were sent out by the church at Antioch. He appealed to his audiences by saying that the field in various foreign lands was ripe unto harvest. He then pled for life, talent, and money for his cause.

He also did much writing for missions. From the pages of the *Gospel Messenger* we note articles on the following subjects: "Doing Our Best for Missions"; "Adam Ebey"; "Our Colleges and Mission Work"; "We Thank You, God Bless You" (after a generous response in giving); "Our Conference Offering"; "Pentecostal Evangelism and Conversion"; "Our Interest in the Conference Budget"; "Showing Faith in Missions"; "Why Not Raise $75,-000 More for the Church? How?"; "Evangelism"; "The Return of the Smiths From China"; "Not Forgotten—S. N. McCann." Repeatedly before Conference he would contribute a short article trying to "boost" the Conference offering.

As was indicated previously, he did a prodigious amount of correspondence concerning missions, not only with the secretaries and other members of the board, but also with missionaries on the field and occasionally with pastors and others who raised questions regarding missions.

Of course, his letters to the field were more often to those whom he had known in college or to older missionaries whom he had learned to know. Many of them had confidence in him and confided in him. To them he often wrote long letters. On February 16, 1922, he wrote to one saying, "Give my regards to Anna and to any inquiring friend. We wrote to the Brights, Mary Shaeffer, Nettie Senger, and have on my desk to answer letters from the

Hershey's and Laura Shock." Many letters from missionaries indicated that they had just received a letter from him.

During a goodly share of his time on the board, President Winger had never been on the mission field. He did not know missions from first-hand experience, nor from extensive study. But he knew people, had a practical mind to know what would work, and, above all, knew the church and her inner spirit.

President and Mrs. Winger visited the mission work in India from March 9 to April 12, 1928. Landing at Bombay, they went north at once through Bulsar to Anklesvar, where President Winger's sister Mabel and her family, the I. W. Moomaws, lived. Since he was the chairman of the General Mission Board he had many official duties to perform. He visited district meetings, at which he usually spoke through an interpreter; he visited the boys' and girls' schools, trade schools, hospitals, and many churches. He observed project work and practice teaching under P. G. Bhagat. He went to Indian villages to observe the work of village evangelists. He got up for early-morning prayer meetings.

In his *Letters from Foreign Lands* he makes observations about the work being done. He discovered many of the same traits of efficiency and inefficiency, of talkativeness or wise restraint, that he knew in Americans.

While in India he made a number of side journeys also, to the famous Woodstock school in the Himalayas, to the Taj Mahal, and to other places of interest.

154

He came away from India feeling that "missions is the greatest and most important work in India today. The only hope for India is the Gospel of Jesus Christ. The missionaries have done a great work in India. They are doing a great work in India today and are worthy of the most liberal support."

He did not share the feeling of some that the Indian Christians could soon carry on the work of the church without the help of missionaries.

India will have need of missionaries and mission money for generations to come. . . . What we have seen in this system of mission stations can be seen all over India, for Christian missions have pretty much covered the land. We are impressed with the infinite need of these people for someone to help them; with the many fine things that the missionaries have done in bringing the Gospel of Jesus Christ to India; with the need and opportunity for the people of America to continue their support of this great work. Missions is the greatest work in India and in the world.

One of the things that annoyed President Winger was the holy men of India. "I am becoming more disgusted with them every day. The most disgusting forms of human filth I have ever seen or dreamed of are to be seen in these unsightly, filthy beings."

He held the Hindu religion responsible for the caste system. He believed this system "blocked all progress and blights all hope." He revolted against it and would have eaten with outcasts had the opportunity presented itself.

He also felt that the wretchedness of Indian womanhood was in no small part the result of the influence of the Hindu religion. "India," said

155

he, "cannot rise until she raises her womanhood." This, he believed, would be achieved through the influence of the Christian faith.

Just what influence his visit to India had on his mission outlook is not easy to determine. Certainly his visit to India and to Moy Gwong's work in South China gave him a more realistic approach to mission work everywhere.

He had a few clear ideas about missions to which he adhered rigidly. He felt that missions abroad should represent the church at home, and that the customs, traditions, and ordinances of the home church should be reproduced in mission fields. At least, the home church should know about any deviation and not be asked to support missions that did not fairly represent the church at home. In one letter he wrote:

> If we cannot run a Dunker Church in a mission field as the church does at home then the church ought to know it. I realize you have some problems. We have them at school but we have pulled the cover off and let folks see. We invite them in. We do not have everything as we used to as we would like to have, neither do the churches. But we have put the matter up to the folks and what support they give, they know to whom and to what it is given. I doubt seriously whether the church will support a mission that has made such changes unless the mission can satisfy the church.

To another missionary he wrote:

> I am sure the missionaries have their problems on the field. We are hoping that in solving the problems in relation to the church . . . the Mission may be kept in close touch with the home church—the home church must know the situation of the field and the mission church must . . . keep the confidence of the home church.

One of the longest, most perplexing problems that arose in the whole time of his service on the board was a matter of personnel on one of the fields. On the issues in this controversy he had strong convictions. Into this controversy he threw himself by correspondence — mostly among board and staff members—with all the vigor of his personality. A small volume of letters was exchanged—long, heated letters at times. But the cause was baffling and bothered the board for several years. When the issues of the controversy did not work out as harmoniously and as he thought they should, he was very much discouraged and expressed to the secretary of the board the feeling that he had failed as chairman of the board and had lost something of self-confidence and enthusiasm. This letter is an unusual letter, and does not really represent his usual spirit.

His contemporaries would say that as a leader in the church and as the chairman of the board he brought to his task on the board a general grasp of the problem and great devotion to it. He was not so open to new projects and points of view as some, but he kept the confidence of the church. His conviction, his frankness, and his honesty were appreciated, as were his frank, direct and incisive decisions.

When he completed his work on the Mission Board, his fellow board members passed the following resolution pertaining to it:

At the recent meeting of the General Mission Board, Otho Winger resigned as chairman after sixteen years of faithful and wise leadership in that position. This was accepted with reluctance and a committee was appointed to make proper record for the Minutes and for the Gospel Messenger. The statement of the Committee follows.

As comrades in a great cause, we as members of the Board desire to pay tribute to the wise counsel and good judgment exercised by our chairman, Brother Otho Winger, through his sixteen years of service as chairman. We desire to record on the Minutes of the General Mission Board and that of the Brethren Publishing House, as well as in the Gospel Messenger, our sincere appreciation of his devotion and fellowship in the work of the church and the world wide interests of the Kingdom of God.

We have been inspired again and again by his dynamic personality, his analytic mind, his penetrating and balanced judgment, his sense of humor and help in difficult problems. While rugged in his convictions of right, he has always with kindliness and sincerity faced the complex situations that such work involves. We recognize the large and unusual place he has filled in our church development. We sincerely assure him of our regret that physical reasons require partial relief from these activities to which he has given himself in the full strength of mind and heart.

Committee:
Rufus D. Bowman
H. H. Nye
C. D. Bonsack

As a Preacher

Otho Winger was elected to the ministry by his home church when he was nineteen and a half year old. He preached his first sermon within a few weeks. From that time until his last sickness he did an enormous amount of preaching. At first it was local, during student days in the Bible Society and the neighboring churches, then in district conference, at Annual Conference, at Sunday-school conventions, and beyond the confines of his own denomination.

At the height of his career, which was probably through the decade of the twenties and the early thirties, he often preached two, three, and four times a Sunday and on other special occasions through the week, and drove two and three hundred miles to do it. He was much in demand to preach dedication sermons, going as far west as the McPherson church in Kansas, and as far east as Pennsylvania and Virginia.

He preached an almost incredible number of funeral sermons far and near. His diary sometimes shows several in a week. Some of these were for people in and around North Manchester, others for people in the region where the college operated, not a few for old neighbors and friends of his old home community, and often for those from outside his own church.

The reason for his demand at funerals is a bit difficult to analyze. He was poised and at ease in these crises; he was extremely tender and sympathetic; and since people liked him and had confidence in him they called upon him in their hour of grief. Then, too, he called at the homes of many sick people. Naturally, when tragedy visited a home, the family often thought of Otho Winger.

He also assisted in a number of Bible institutes at various places on college campuses, in district gatherings, and in individual churches.

Reviewing his diary for the year 1924, we discover that there are recorded one hundred twenty-five addresses, of which fifteen were funeral sermons and twelve were commencement addresses.

One gets an idea of the range of his travels to do this speaking by mentioning the towns in which it was done. All these places are mentioned in the diary for 1924: Indianapolis; Wabash; Plymouth; Bourbon; La Porte; Roann; Defiance, Ohio; West Alexandria, Ohio; South Whitley; Gilead; Brookville, Ohio; Knox; Middlebury; Pitsburg, Ohio; Franklin Grove, Illinois; Syracuse; Jewell, Ohio; Nappanee; Mexico; Monticello; Huntington; Peru; Goshen; Sidney, Ohio; Hagerstown; Garrett; Parsons, Kansas; Michigan City; Zanesville, Ohio; Juniata College, Pennsylvania; Elizabethtown College, Pennsylvania. All these places were touched, many of them more than once in this one year. As early as October 15, 1916, his diary says, "At home for the first time in twelve weeks on Sunday."

To these places he traveled in an old Ford for many years. His rate of travel was terrific. Sometimes one feared the Ford would fly to pieces. Uphill, downhill, through all kinds of weather, he drove like Jehu. Sometimes crashing through wire fences or against trains, killing a horse, or colliding with other cars, he drove day and night. He once said to the writer that his motto was not to do anything to a Ford as long as it would run. When the men in the town of North Manchester bought him his new Buick he accepted it gratefully and drove it with the same incredible speed. In his diary he wrote, "Buick is doing fine but not fast enough yet."

In his *Memories of Manchester* he says he

preached more than sixty church dedications. He had part in district meetings of his home district before he went to college, and for a period of twenty-four years he did not miss a single district conference; he served occasionally as moderator. As was mentioned earlier, during the twenty-five years between 1911 and 1936, he did not miss a single Annual Conference.

He was a forceful preacher. The strength of his preaching probably lay in the force of his personality, in his marvelous and contagious enthusiasm, in his clarity of mind, and his good, common-sense judgment.

He did not make great effort for nicety of language and expression; nor did he resort to any of the tricks or devices of the polished orator. In fact, his sermons while powerful and often very convincing did not show evidence of careful preparation. He was too much of an activist for that. They often showed signs of having been hastily put together, and consisted of materials gleaned in the actual experiences of his crowded life. He had a marvelous memory and often he drew heavily from history and literature for materials.

But, even so, he was a popular preacher and in great demand. Whatever his sermons lacked in the above-mentioned respects was compensated for by the force and enthusiasm of the preacher, by the depth of his conviction, and by the winsomeness of his personality.

His sermons were occasionally doctrinal. From a group of some seventy-five outlines left in the archives, we find such doctrinal subjects as *The*

Doctrine of God; The Doctrine of Man; The Devil; The Bible; The Church; Regeneration, Grace; What Is Truth? Obedience; Stewardship; Truth and Symbols; Pentecostal Evangelism.

Most of his sermons were of a practical or inspirational nature; many were of a hortatory type. These were full of practical illustrations as well as literary and historical references.

In the sermon outlines before me I find such topics as *Open and Closed Doors; The Urgency of Life; Strength; Redeeming the Time; Joshua; The Simple Life; Witnessing for Christ; Jesus Christ and the Church in Community; Our Crisis; Courage and Hope; Looking Forward; The Greatest Thing in the World; Non-conformity; Our Outlook in Life; The More Abundant Life; The Second Mile; The Mission of Life; The Voyage of Life; Two Boys (the Prodigal Son).*

His sermon outlines were brief, being usually on both sides of one sheet of notepaper three and three-fourths by six and one-fourth inches in size. Sometimes they ran to two sheets. Most of them show signs of considerable use, with marginal jottings and interlinear notations.

During most of his life his sermons were positive, forward looking, hopeful, and inspiring. In his later years there sometimes crept into them a note of the disappointment he felt at some of the trends in society and in the church. Then, too, occasionally he was tempted to scold and to denounce more than formerly.

But all in all, he was a great preacher, great because of the depth of his convictions, the largeness of his vision, the devotion and unselfishness of his life, and the overwhelming power of his great personality. To quote Edward Frantz, "he looked and talked like a leader." And when Brethren anywhere had an important occasion for which they wanted a great preacher, very often they sent for Otho Winger.

As a "Pastor" or Home Visitor

Not a little of the influence of Otho Winger was exercised by his home visitation. His early habit of visiting the sick continued through life. Doctor Perry, a North Manchester physician, said that often when he was called to a home on account of sickness he found that Otho Winger had already been there. This was a deeply ingrained habit and seemed perfectly natural to him. It included in its scope sick students, members of his family, neighbors, or friends at some distance. His visits were usually not long but were genial, pleasant, sympathetic, and hopeful. He left behind him a glow of deep appreciation in the life of the one visited.

For a time, while there was no pastor at the Walnut Street church in North Manchester, Otho Winger was elder-in-charge. He wrote in his diary in April 1922, "The Church work lays near my heart and without a pastor this year, the responsibility for so large a church is not small—sermons, funerals, baccalaureate, commencements, all great opportunities."

During this time his diary has notes like the following: "February 26, 1922, Sunday sermons by

L. D. Ikenberry, and H. S. Randolph. Visited in homes of J. H. Wright, P. E. Grossnickle, Henry Wilson, George Martin, Levi Forney, Joseph Neher, Mary Early, A. C. Mote." Even when the church had a pastor President Winger's home visitation continued. His diary for 1924 is filled with reports of visits in the homes of the community. On January 6 he visited nine families and boys in the dormitory; January 13, six families; January 20, three families; January 27, five families; February 3, seven families; November 16, twelve families; November 27, twelve families. On November 30 he "visited many homes in the country." On August 9, 1925, he preached at the Walnut Street church and made calls at twenty-five places during the day.

His Role in the Church of the Brethren

Otho Winger's national recognition and leadership in the Church of the Brethren can be said to have extended roughly from about 1911 to 1941. The period up to 1911 was one of preparation and apprenticeship. His national recognition began at the opening of the second decade of the century.

This period was an interesting and significant period in the history of the Church of the Brethren. Through the nineteenth century the church had followed the policy of withdrawing from the world. The persecutions of the war times and the church's distinctive doctrines and practices, especially as to dress, led the church to withdraw from the cities and centers of population. She became largely rural and lived a life more or less apart from the general stream of public life.

Up to 1875, there was no college which had enough public support to survive. The leadership of the church was largely in the hands of a lay ministry most of whom had no higher educational training, or if they had any they had secured it outside the church. A very large percentage of her membership were farmers or tradesmen. They took little part in politics and in the popular pleasures of the day.

But the church began to break away from this isolation and separation during the latter decades of the nineteenth century and the early days of the twentieth. Little by little the walls of separation began to give way. More people moved to the cities. Young men and women went into higher education in colleges. Brethren went into business. More Brethren took up teaching and other "secular" activities. Here and there, there were folks in the church who ventured to discard the distinctive dress of the church.

Moreover, in the late nineteen hundreds, colleges were founded by the church: Juniata in 1875, Mount Morris in 1878, McPherson in 1887, Manchester in 1895. Higher education was beginning to get some support from the church, though many still held college as suspect, feeling that college people were likely to become proud and worldly.

It was in the period of the active leadership of Otho Winger that we see the church gradually breaking away from her isolation and taking her place in the general stream of the public life of America. It was also the period when the church waged a long, difficult, and only partially successful battle to maintain her distinctiveness in dress, in forms of worship, and in "separation from the world." It was, as we have seen elsewhere, the period of the great growth and popularization of higher education in America. Scarcely any of our colleges were assured of their survival until 1910. After that several of them grew rapidly and became strong.

It was during this period that the church was gradually making a transition from a so-called free

166

ministry to a part-time or full-time professionally trained ministry. This change did not come without controversy and a great deal of heartache on the part of both the free ministers and the full-time pastors as well as the congregations they served.

It was the era of higher criticism. This led to the fundamentalist-modernist controversy which has bedeviled American Protestantism for more than a quarter-century. President Winger naturally could not hope to escape getting involved in this discussion.

The period from 1907, when he came to Manchester to teach, to 1941, when he retired from the presidency of the college, also saw the expansion of the use of the automobile, the development of the moving picture industry, the coming of the radio, the invention and the extensive use of the airplane, and a multitude of other inventions for home and industry. All of these affected the tone and temper of American social life, its ideals and its practices. It was, in brief, what we have come to know as the period of the vast secularization of American life and thought.

It was the period in the general church life of America of emphasis on the social gospel which sensitized the public to the evils in our society, such as race discrimination, economic injustice, intemperance, and war. Out of this emphasis grew a number of social service organizations, various peace movements, and temperance organizations.

Moreover, the period from 1895 to about 1940 was the great period of foreign missions in the church. Christian Hope in the late seventies had started a small awakening of interest in missions in Denmark and Sweden. But it was not until about 1895, when Wilbur Stover and his wife, along with Bertha Ryan, went to India fresh from the campus of Mount Morris College, that the missionary movement in the Church of the Brethren took on significant proportions. From the end of the nineteenth century through the first four decades of the twentieth century, foreign missions was considered "the great first-work of the church," to use a phrase coined by Wilbur Stover. Missions rode the crest of the wave of public interest. The church had a strong board to direct this work. Some of the best and most consecrated young men and women volunteered for service in foreign fields. It was the movement that seemed to represent the acme of spiritual consecration. It was during most of this period that Otho Winger was active on the Mission Board and served his sixteen years as chairman.

It is commonly accepted that President Otho Winger was one of a small group of strong men who held the Church of the Brethren together during these troublous transition days. That is, these men, most of whom were in educational work and in sympathy with the best in education, were also so completely identified with the church in her faith, her ideals, and her practices that they held the confidence of the masses of non-educational people and thus kept the groups together and led the church forward.

Let us see if we can determine the position of Otho Winger on some of the questions that confronted the church during his career.

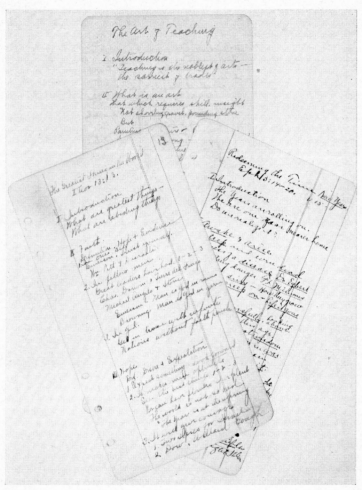

Samples of His Sermon Outlines

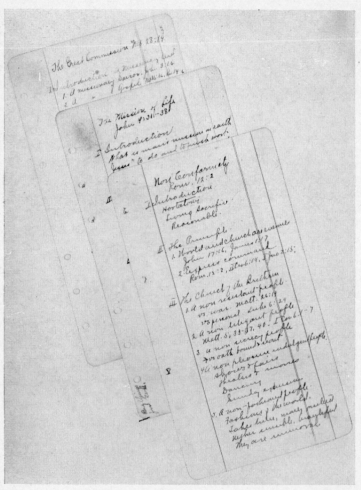

Samples of His Sermon Outlines

His position on many questions may be discovered in his sermons, his chapel talks, his discussions at Annual Conference, his reports to the college trustees, and most of all in his letters. The most revealing letters are those to some of his intimate co-workers and to people who had written to him for advice and counsel on specific religious questions. We shall let him speak for himself on some of these issues.

Before presenting his viewpoints, however, it seems fair to say that he did not consider himself a theologian. In his address as a fraternal relations delegate to the Progressive Brethren at Winona Lake in about 1933 he said:

> I am a layman when it comes to theology, and I think I represent very much the viewpoint of the average layman or member of the church, who is interested in the teaching of the Bible but not so much interested in theological discussion. Expert theologians may get confused and wrought up over some nice distinctions, but even in times like this the great body of our people stand firm on the teachings of the Bible and strong in the faith of their fathers.

It is not entirely true that he was uninformed on theological questions, but he certainly had slight interest in the hair-splitting distinctions that theologians often make. Some of his critics regretted his lack of what they called "theological insight." It was not so much lack of insight as lack of interest in these divisive controversies that influenced him.

We will first note his position on some of the more general questions of religious faith which concerned not only the Brethren but all churches.

In 1932 in answer to questions regarding the creation and certain other doctrines he wrote:

On the creation of man, I believe that God created him just as the Bible says. I believe that man fell through sin and that the only thing that is able to bring him back into full fellowship with God, is the redeeming blood of Jesus Christ. Of justification by faith, of course, I believe in it, whatever the Bible teaches on it. . . . But if it means carelessness in doing good work and obedience, then I would have to modify. I believe in heaven and could scarcely believe in it unless I believed in hell also.

In answer to another letter during the same year he wrote concerning Jesus Christ:

As I understand, the Bible teaches that Jesus Christ was what his name signifies—God in humanity. That is, in the person of Jesus Christ, God and man combine. The ancient church decided . . . that Jesus Christ was perfect God and perfect man, that he had a perfect divine nature, and a perfect human nature and that these two were perfectly united. On the one hand he had the attributes of deity. These he claimed and on many occasions he manifested his divine power. On the other hand he was perfectly human and so he would understand all human experiences as well. As a human being he was subject to temptations, but these he conquered and through him men can conquer, but this doesn't exclude that he was also divine.

President Winger also often in addresses spoke on this question used in our Brethren baptismal vows: "Do you believe that Jesus Christ was the Son of God and that he brought from Heaven a saving gospel?" His affirmative answer to this question was, I think, one of the major planks of his personal faith. In a number of his sermons he used the three questions usually presented to candidates for baptism as an outline for his sermon. This was one of them and on it he often preached.

A certain woman wrote to President Winger telling of the worldliness in her church and wondered whether it might not help to preach the doctrine of the second coming of Christ. To this inquiry he replied:

Of course, we should preach it. It is one of the great Bible truths and one of the great hopes that the Christian has. The only difficulty I have in this is that some people have been carried away with this or that interpretation of the second coming and neglected the more important things of life; of course, it is true that our Lord may come at any time—today or before the close of the month or year, but nevertheless he hasn't told us when he is coming. . . . It is our business to witness till he comes again.

He then sums up his advice to the sister by saying: "Let your faith and hope in God's word be bright; look for the coming of our Lord, as all Christians should and do; but do your best to witness for Him and set the best example possible."

In other cases when people wrote him about the second coming he repeated his faith in the doctrine but often told some of those who wrote about it that they were talking beyond their knowledge, that Jesus had emphatically said that "no man knoweth the day nor the hour."

In the midst of the fundamentalist-modernist controversy he had many occasions to speak or write on the question. If talking to or about liberals or modernists he spoke out boldly and often vehemently against those who were inclined to disturb the faith of others by teaching what was questionable. He classified himself as a fundamentalist but defined what he meant by fundamentalism. In answer to a critical letter from one of his college constituents, he said:

I want to say just a word about the so-called fundamentalism. First, I want it understood that so far as that name applies to doctrine I agree with them [the fundamentalists]. I doubt whether any of them have taught the fundamental teachings much longer and much more strongly than I have. I haven't done it from policy. I have done it from conviction. . . . I believe in the fundamental teachings of Jesus Christ, and doctrinally, I believe in all that fundamentalists teach so far as it relates to doctrine. But they have developed an attitude of mind which I believe is entirely wrong. Unless you believe in their interpretation in everything, you are entirely wrong.

There can be no question that President Winger was nearer in his doctrinal position to the fundamentalists than to the so-called modernists, but it is also true that he was too much a man of action to give place to hair-splitting theological controversy that divided the church and blocked progress.

In answer to an inquiry about the doctrine of evolution he wrote:

I do not accept the evolution doctrine. I do not believe it. I have told every class of mine that for twenty years. The evolutionists say a lot of things they do not know. Then, others make a lot of deductions from the doctrines that are worse yet. I have only one answer to the origin of man; that is the Bible answer. God made him and breathed into his nostrils the breath of life and man became a living soul. That is all I know about it. What I want to know is that man is a child of God and has the hope of an immortal existence with Him,

In regard to miracles he said: "I believe in the miracles as recorded in the New Testament. I have no reason not to believe them. I have no disposition to explain them away. I take them at their face value."

We shall now indicate his position on certain questions pertaining to the distinctive doctrines and practices of the Church of the Brethren. It is well, while doing this, to remember that he sprang out of a plain but substantial Dunker home. He grew up in a small, conservative country church. His church was probably typical of most of the Dunker churches of his region and of many other parts of the United States. His training and background was that of a typical Dunker. We shall discover that he was loyal to the doctrines, the ideals, and the practices of the church.

The following is a letter written by President Winger in 1922 which has been used heretofore in another connection, but which better than anything he has written defines his attitude toward the church of his choice, his attitude toward her teachings, and his viewpoint regarding a member who ceases to believe them.

. . . I was raised a Dunker. I have accepted her principles and policies. I have promised to teach and practice them and have accepted my office and responsibility on that ground, and when I cannot continue I shall state the matter plainly to the church and resign unless she wants me to continue. Further from conviction, I believe that the Bible teaches these things and while I recognize that these ordinances teach greater truths than the forms, I believe that Jesus knew what he was doing. And while I have the greatest tolerance for folks of other churches who are sincere, I believe that there is needed a people who in simplicity follows the plain teachings and example of our Lord.

Let us amplify on this general statement made by him regarding the church, her practices, and her teachings.

As evidence that he tried to teach these distinctive doctrines in the college we have the following item in the trustee minutes in 1921:

On motion in view of the fact of the need of teaching of the simple life among all people, and especially among members of the church, be it known that we the present trustees of Manchester College do indorse and commend President Winger and his co-workers for their attitude and effort to encourage the simple life in the student body.

In his report to the trustees on March 27, 1936, he said: "We would like to have an expression of the trustees on some of the popular pleasures of the day, such as dancing and card playing. The management has been standing for the time honored position of our church on this question. What do you say?" To this the trustees replied by approving the time-honored position regarding popular amusements and indulgences such as "dancing, card playing, cigarette smoking and 'boose.'"

We have already seen that during his early period he opposed the use of the piano in the church and made an address against it on the floor of Annual Conference. In a letter in 1921, he wrote: "As far as music instruments are concerned: I do not like them in church services. There is no scripture against them, that I know of, but I am not in favor of using it for I don't believe we can retain the spirit and fullness of song, as we can if we enter into it without." Of course, he had a piano in his home and encouraged his boys to learn to play it.

In the same letter he reports on the issue of membership in lodges: "It is not permitted Brethren to hold membership in either 'secret or oath bound' societies. The report passed in 1926 makes that clear enough. Our church has always been clear on this and should continue to be so."

It had long been the practice of the church to ask women to wear a veil during religious services in conformity to Paul's teaching in First Corinthians 11. Any practice that sets a group off as different from the common practice is always difficult to maintain. A number of people wrote to President Winger asking his opinion and teaching on it. In 1927 and again in 1933 he wrote: "I have no doubt whatever that the scriptures teach that women should be veiled in public worship." There are other practices of the church on which he may have changed his opinion or on which he accepted the new practice, such as the use of the piano. There is no evidence that he changed his conviction on the prayer veil.

To an inquirer regarding the practice of women bobbing their hair he wrote: "I am in full accord with the decision of the late annual conference which said, 'The worldly custom of women wearing bobbed hair is contrary to scripture and Christian modesty, and we urge all our sisters to adorn themselves as women professing godliness.'"

President Winger was not sympathetic with

the use of tobacco, but he was more tolerant and forbearing with college boys who had the habit than were some of his faculty. But that he talked vigorously against tobacco is attested to by the following anonymous letter which came to him early in his presidency. There was a rule that people who raised or used tobacco could not serve as delegates to district conference or Annual Conference. The women who wrote this letter resented President Winger's references to tobacco raisers, hence the letter.

Dayton, Ohio, April 29, 1915   Personal to
    Mr. Otho Winger—   Dear Bro.—

    In speaking with a number of Brethren and Sister in regard to the unjust queries of District Meeting of Southern Ohio as brought before a few chosen ones to be decided on and increase our taxation which we claim is very unjust and tyrannical (as a large number or majority of the members of the Miami Valley have no say as they raise or have raised tobacco.) and speaking we decided to write you because of some of the remarks you made at the Institute at Dayton. and you can think it over, you classed it with a Barroom. If so why don't you make it a test of fellowship and throw us out or make us quit. you leaders are a pack of cowards and the money hurts you. We say out with the hell trafic as you called it. pretty strong, back it up. you cowardly accusiers. our Husbands are farmers and as good as the cowardly College professors who can come out and abuse us hard working people. take off your gloves get out and dig. no you fellows like to whistle and we come with our money and fatten your Mission calls with Tobacco money yet you think the Tobacco raiser and the saloon keeper equal. yet you claim thousands as your brethren when you want money. and sees them just the same yet not represented at AM. or Dist. Meeting. If they are not your Brethren at these meetings you just want their money. this is a fact and you are too cowardly to own your own guilt not only you but all with you. somebody is going to come short. how about Mat. 18.18 out with your supposed sin we are getting sick of your howling. why don't you do something? I could get you Hundreds of subscribers but we dont count on decisions so we dare you, fire ahead not over your shoulder. blow your bugle get the other brave fellows. march along, get busy now.

On the envelope containing this letter he had written, "A scoring for talking vs. tobacco." One can imagine him having a good laugh over this vehement comeback.

It has already been noted that Otho Winger, until after 1926, repeatedly opposed the appointment of a Fraternal Relations Committee to try to re-establish relationships with the Progressive Brethren Church. Up to that time he felt that any effort to reunite with this so-called liberal group might result in losing a large wing of the conservatives. After 1926 he favored making a reasonable effort to reunite. His attitude on this issue was clearly set forth in a letter to H. C. Early in 1933.

It has also been noted that President Winger was most influential in the 1926 Annual Conference at Lincoln, Nebraska, when the church was threatened by a split led by B. E. Kessler of Poplar Ridge, Missouri, and others. He had the confidence of the conservatives and used his leadership to soften the report of Conference so as not to lose the more liberal group while attempting to satisfy the conservatives. In the report he presented to Annual Conference at that time, the work of his own hand, he took a position against secret orders, against immodest dress, jewelry, worldly amusements, and bobbed hair. He advocated the faithful teaching of the simple life, the revival of the family altar, spiritual worship services, the use of the Lord's Prayer, the kneeling posture in prayer, the salutation of the holy kiss, and that "we renew our vows of love for the Church of the Brethren and for one another." His work at this Conference he himself regarded as most important in preventing a major division in the church.

To sum up his position in the church, it can safely be said that any intimate study of the life of Otho Winger convinces one that he held the generally accepted orthodox views regarding the great Christian doctrines held by most Protestant churches of his day and that he accepted, practiced, and taught the distinctive (some would say *peculiar*) doctrines and practices of the Church of the Brethren.

He was strong in his belief that a Christian should be different from the world in appearance, in purity of life, and in social relationships.

While his attitude may make him seem separatist in a sense, he was not entirely so. He was tolerant and friendly to all. He lived true to his own convictions, but made his impact on the society of his day, still holding to his distinctive doctrines and practices.

One of President Winger's critics points out that his ethics changed with the changes of Annual Meeting minutes. Would it not be more accurate and also kinder to say that on matters of policy and church practices he seemed to think it better to

stay by the decisions of the church until those decisions were changed than to disregard them and
thus lead to chaotic conditions? It is possible that
to some who were in a hurry for certain changes in
the church he seemed like a hindrance. There are
perhaps instances in which he opposed changes
which might have been for the better, but for the
most part the things he opposed were trends toward
"compromise" with the world and laxity of standards.

Then, too, it seemed to be his conviction that
it was more important to keep unity in the church
and to keep the church going forward together on
its work of evangelism, missions, and other issues
of importance than to relax its requirements for
church membership.

In his later years—in the late nineteen thirties—
President Winger was deeply disappointed in certain worldly trends in the church. The following is
his own review of an address he had given at Troy,
Ohio, written when someone asked him for a copy
of the address.

There is no doubt that there is a great laxity on
the part of our homes and on the part of our ministry
in some of the evils that beset society today. There was
a time when we seemed to be very strict as a church and
as a people, but our strictness was largely along the line
of dress. When we had to let loose of that, it seemed as
though we let loose of almost everything. I am not one
who thinks that the young folks of today are worse than
they used to be. I do not think they are; but I do think
they have more temptations than they used to have. The
young man or the young woman who lives right today has
more credit than those who lived right a generation ago,
because they have more temptations. True, there must

179

have been temptations and the possibility of sinning, but I do not think it ever pursued young folks as much as it does now. I have just written a letter to the president of another college on the question of dancing. We do not have the problem in our college very much as yet, but it is a wonder if we don't, because society everywhere is engaging in it, and many of our own members are engaging in it without any compunction of conscience. The same thing is true of card playing. But that isn't all.

There have undoubtedly been great temptations to laxity on morals in general. It isn't a secret at all that there are people and organizations who claim that even our old-time care of sexual purity is all bunk, that men and women have a right to live in any way that will give expression to their desires and emotions. That is pretty common in some sections among old as well as young. There are a great many young people who are exposed to the temptation of that kind of conduct in the community in which they live. We have students here that tell us that that is true in their communities.

Now we have been trying to work with these problems. We have always tried to work with the church, even when the church had some rather stricter regulations. We are still trying to do that. I think sometimes we are doing more than most pastors and elders are. Some things we don't permit here that are freely permitted in the homes or home communities. I think we are a little more concerned about the conduct than many homes and many pastors are. My attitude on this is not one of quarreling with young folks about their conduct, but of having some convictions of our own and teaching those things to the youth and trying to get them to see the beauty of the good life. We believe that after all the virtuous life is something to be achieved as a thing of beauty and that it is appealing yet to young men and women, but when older folks lose their concern and their convictions about these matters and are afraid to say anything about them we cannot expect our youth to be

concerned. I am not saying that older people, parents
and pastors, can prevent some of these things, but I do
say that we have a tremendous responsibility in having
some convictions of right and in teaching these convictions to others.

In a letter of discouragement written to a close
friend regarding the increasing laxity in the church,
he reviewed the trend toward card playing, dancing,
sex freedom, nudity in camps, and bathing beaches.
But the matter that troubled him most was the lack
of faithfulness and courage on the part of preachers
and other leaders to speak against these evils in the
church. Some, he felt, were leading the church
toward greater worldliness or at least were doing
little to keep the church from worldliness.

"Personally," said he, "I doubt whether there
is a denomination in the world that is going faster
toward worldliness and a form of Christian pagan-
ism than our own church."

At another time he said:

I am trying with all my heart to keep faith in our
church leaders, but it is not easy to be always optimistic.
We have some stalwart Christian missionaries. We have
some great coming Christian leaders. But there are others
whose attitudes give me great concern. I hope I am
wrong. I hope this is just my liver. But this is my present impression which I am just saying to you. I suppose
I will feel better when I get it off my chest.

It seems to the author that it is difficult for a
man to be a general and a creative statesman. In
some sense President Winger was both. But he
sometimes seems more like a general trying to keep
the troops organized and marching forward together
than a creative statesman.

181

Otho Winger was a member of the General Educational Board of the Church of the Brethren from 1911 to 1915, and again from about 1926 to 1941. He was president of Manchester College from 1911 to 1941. He was a member of the General Mission Board from 1912 to 1943. Between 1915 and 1935 he was reading clerk of Annual Conference three times and moderator six times. Besides, he helped revise the minutes of the Annual Conference and held other lesser short-time positions in the church.

That he stood at a vantage point to affect the life of the church in a powerful way for a period of thirty years is evident. No weak man would be elected to all these responsible positions. A strong man in all these positions of influence is bound to make a deep impress and do much to help determine its direction.

That he greatly promoted the interest of missions and Manchester College is beyond question. That he set forward the general program of the church in many ways would be quite generally conceded. He was influential in getting the Brethren people to accept higher education, he promoted home and foreign missions among the churches, he encouraged Christian education in the Sunday school, he gave support to a salaried ministry, he co-operated with and encouraged the seminary movement, he promoted the general church life in his area and beyond, and he was a mighty force for good living among thousands of students.

A. C. Wieand says of him:

I have never understood the life and mission of Brother Winger until I saw him, mingling intimately

182

with the rank and file of the elders of Indiana, and Ohio, the men who were the wheel horses and key men in those regions. This great educator, in the humblest and most intimate fellowship which came very close to the lives and work of these ministers of the churches. Perhaps no man ever mingled more intimately with so many of the churches, or so many of the members in the Manchester College area as did Brother Winger. He was acquainted with all their problems. He knew all their leaders and most of the young people. They looked up to him. They relied on him for his judgment and sympathy, his great interest, his unbiased judgment and unselfish service.

Otho Winger, as we have seen, accepted the basic doctrines and practices of the Church of the Brethren very much as he found them as a young man. He believed that there was needed a people "who in simplicity follows the plain teaching and example of our Lord."

He believed that Jesus knew what he was doing when he established some of the distinctive rites followed by the church. He believed Paul meant that his teaching in First Corinthians 11 should become universal. He believed that card playing, dancing, and other related practices sapped the spiritual life of the church and should be avoided. He said, "Pride, worldliness, lack of faith in God's word, willful refusal to obey God's law, these and many others I condemn." There can be little question that his influence tended to stabilize the church and hold it true to its historic practices, because he thought it was right to do so and because he thought that many of the innovations were harmful to the best interests of the church.

There were others in the church who felt that some of the distinctive practices of the church were not fundamental to salvation, and were a hindrance to the growth of the church. They wanted change. Many wanted to eliminate the distinctive dress of both men and women, some wanted pianos in the churches before the majority of the church members were ready for them, some wanted to repeal the anti-secrecy clause in our regulations, and others would eliminate certain parts of the communion service. That some of these were sincere is, doubtless, evident. Perhaps others joined them for motives not so high.

Against some of these innovations Otho Winger took a strong stand. With his strong influence he sometimes delayed or blocked these movements. It would be natural for those so blocked to say that he hindered progress, while to "the defenders of the faith" he was a hero and a "safe" leader. Whether delay in the coming of the piano into the church and delay in certain other changes in the church was a hindrance can perhaps be determined by our judgment of how much improvement they have brought to the church since their coming. That he did much to keep the church together and at work at certain worthy activities such as missions, education, evangelism, we have shown on other pages.

But the trends of the times militated mightily against the distinctive practices and the high ideals that President Winger had set for the church. When he was a lad the church was still very much "separatist." It was not so difficult to maintain distinctiveness. But with the popularization of the public high school, the common use of the auto, the coming of the movie and the radio, and the increasing urbanization of life it became very difficult to maintain a level of life in church or college higher than the social life of the general community and a distinctiveness in dress and social practices different from those of the community.

That there was a vast secularization of life especially after the First World War is known to all. That worldliness in the sense he used the term was on the increase cannot be questioned. Just how much less spiritual the church was is not easy to determine. Conditions were such, however, as to make him exceedingly unhappy. Perhaps his ideals for the church were too difficult for the masses. St. Francis and others have been able to raise up groups who defied public sentiment and lived above it, but they were a choice few. "Bigness" on the one hand and high levels of spiritual life and practice demanding folks to be "different" seem incompatible. Only the select attain great heights of spiritual life. Only a few will dare to be different for the sake of an ideal.

It is the conviction of the writer that on the negative side he did use his influence to delay certain innovations in church practices, but that on the positive side he did much on the side of keeping the church busy at the "King's business," that he was influential in holding the church together when it was threatened with division, and that he was a power for righteousness wherever his influence was felt.

185

Otho Winger as a Traveler

Those who knew Otho Winger as a college president wondered how he had any time to give to the church. Those who knew of his varied and extensive activities in the church wondered when he had any time to direct a college. Those who knew of his writings wondered when he had time to do much else. Certainly those who knew of his activities in school and church and as an author did not realize that he also did much traveling.

For a man who was for forty-one years a teacher, and for thirty of these years a college president, he was an extensive traveler. His travels began when he was quite young and continued throughout his life. He visited every state in the Union—many of them frequently. He traveled in Canada. He and Mrs. Winger went around the world in 1927 and 1928—mostly during the first six months of 1928. On this journey he visited England, France, Belgium, Holland, Denmark, Sweden, Germany, Switzerland, Italy, Greece, Turkey, Palestine, Egypt, India, China, Japan, and Hawaii, returning by way of California.

He attended the Annual Conference of his church almost yearly during most of his active life, never missing from 1911 to 1936. In his *Tribute to Ida Miller Winger* he said: "We generally chose those routes that would take us into territory where

186

we had not been, and thus we got to see a great deal of the United States."

President Winger had wide interest and a keen intellectual curiosity. He was interested in people, the way they lived and worked and the way they thought. He wanted to know the leading facts about the countries in which he traveled and about the cities he visited. He had been a teacher of history and of literature. His memory was most remarkable, and as he visited historic places he could recall what had happened there or what the poets had said about the place. These historic and literary references appear in his diaries and his writings.

He was always an activist; he was never a quietist. He investigated and examined for himself. What others had done he would do; what was to be seen and experienced he would see and experience for himself. On their honeymoon to Niagara in 1902, he and Mrs. Winger rode on the Maid of the Mist, even though to do so was dangerous. When he visited the Grand Canyon, it was not enough to stand on the banks and look into the giant gorge; he mounted a huge donkey and rode seven miles down to the Colorado River. When he got to Boston late at night and had found his hotel, he wrote in his notes, "A little walk on the streets—then to bed—a good nights sleep." His notes, written in Berlin, disparage the value of a sight-seeing tour by bus, which whirls one around and leaves him but a confused picture; he says, "Since we have but a short time for Berlin we are going to walk to see a few things well."

After arriving in Venice he wrote: "When our luggage is in the room our curiosity is too great for us to remain here until morning so we ask whether there is a way to walk down town. You can walk almost anywhere in Venice. So we step into a narrow street and find it full of people." Of the next morning after arriving at Jerusalem he said: "We cannot resist the temptation to take an early walk within the walls." Later he wrote, "Having walked through most of the streets, some of them again and again. . . ." After having gone in and out of all its gates and after visiting some of the most interesting places a number of times he described the city. Then he added, "It is interesting to walk around the city outside its walls. We have had many such walks and once we set out and walked around the whole city." When he got to the five-hundred-feet-high Egyptian pyramids with steps four and five feet high he climbed to the top of one of them "with the help of two Arabs, one pushing and another pulling." Moreover, after he had climbed to the top of the pyramid he descended and entered it and went through dark, low passageways to the king's tomb, and then to the queen's tomb, then "we retrace our steps and reach the open air, glad for the experience but not caring to repeat it."

In Greece he climbed to the Acropolis, viewing its scenes and reviewing its history. Then he went to Mars Hill and sat there recalling that it was the place where Socrates had been tried and where Paul had preached. Here they sat down and read Paul's address delivered on Mars Hill.

In India, China, and Japan he walked where others were carried or where they were pulled by coolies in jinrikishas. In China he walked the narrow roads between the watery rice fields—roads so narrow that one brushed against the oxen as they passed.

It is remarkable, too, in how many countries he managed in some way to get into a home to eat with the common people. In London he spent an hour in the home of Mrs. Jennie Weber and had tea with her and her family. In Sweden he and Pastor Graybill called at two Swedish homes.

I cannot talk this language but find the people very polite. . . . At or near the village of Simrishamn I have my first visit in a Swedish country home. It is only ten o'clock but we must eat with them. They set out a cold lunch and hot coffee. They call it only a lunch but here are three different kinds of meat, and four different kinds of cake to be eaten with the coffee. . . . The homes of these people seem cheery, but their churches are barren.

At Schwarzenau he wrote, "We do not get to visit in any homes but from what we can see somewhere in each of these homes they must keep a cow or two. At least the cow quarters are under the same roof with the family. When spring comes and the straw and refuse are moved to yonder fields no doubt these streets will be beautiful, but not now." In Egypt he ate in the home of an Arab Bedouin and got to see the home. In Palestine he got into the home of his Arab Mohammedan guide. In India and China he had no difficulty in getting into homes. This happened also in Japan and no doubt elsewhere of which we have no record.

As one reads President Winger's diaries, he is impressed with the suddenness with which he is off for a journey. Out of a busy life of school activities and of public arrangements, all at once he would suddenly be off for some long journey. However, his son Paul says that before going on their trip around the world his father and mother had studied the places they were to visit, and before he left Fort Wayne his father knew exactly what he wanted to see in each country they were to visit. When someone asked them whether they had gone on a conducted tour of Europe, Mr. Winger answered no, but Mrs. Winger's answer was yes.

The same intensity with which he did his work at the college entered into his travels. On their trips to Conference and their trips to Florida, the Southwest, Kansas, Oklahoma, Texas, Louisiana, Tennessee, or elsewhere in pursuit of Indian history, on which longer trips Mrs. Winger usually accompanied him, he sometimes made terrificly hard drives. In one of Mrs. Winger's diary or record books she recorded three hundred seventy-one miles the first day, Sunday, four hundred seventy-nine miles the second day, and four hundred fifty miles the third day. On this journey J. O. was along and probably did part of the driving. On another journey President Winger recorded two hundred miles after 5:00 p.m., two hundred forty-five miles in an afternoon, four hundred thirty-eight miles, four hundred forty-six miles, six hundred miles, and still another six hundred miles.

One of the interesting journeys recorded by both Mr. and Mrs. Winger began on November 3,

1935, by way of Chicago and Elgin, where there were board meetings from Monday until 3:30 p.m., on Wednesday. They went on to Springfield, Illinois, for the night, to Hannibal, Missouri, for breakfast, to Cameron, Missouri, for dinner (there they could not find a place to eat without beer; so they went to a grocery store and got apples, buns, and candy), then to Haskell Institute outside Lawrence, Kansas, for the night. Here Otho went to the library for his Indian history; here he met many Indians and talked with them about their people. From Lawrence they went through the Ozarks to Dallas, Falfurrias, and Brownsville, Texas. They took a bus trip into Old Mexico.

On their return they came through Brownsville and Corpus Christi, Texas. At Welsh, Louisiana, they visited friends, the Hoke family. From here to Baton Rouge and New Orleans, Louisiana; Ocean Springs, Mississippi; Mobile and Citronelle (where Mrs. Winger had once taught), Alabama; Pensacola, Florida; Montgomery and Birmingham, Alabama; Athens, Georgia; Muscle Shoals and Florence, Tennessee; Columbia, South Carolina; Nashville, Tennessee; Louisville, Kentucky; Indianapolis, Kokomo, and home. They rode six hundred miles on Friday, Mrs. Winger said. They had traveled five thousand miles in all, and were gone twenty-one nights, of which they spent ten with friends, six at tourist courts, and five in hotels. They had been in twelve states besides Indiana.

On the trip referred to above and on other trips Otho spent an occasional half-day or day in some library pursuing his Indian studies. On a trip to

Florida he stopped in Washington and did research in the Library of Congress. If in Chicago he spent time in the John Crearer Library. During his research Mrs. Winger would sew, crochet, do some shopping, or just rest in her hotel room.

In the summer of 1922, soon after the closing activities of the college year and a long list of high school commencements, the opening of the summer term, the death of his father on June 5, and Annual Conference at Winona Lake, Otho Winger left home to attend the National Educational Association meetings in Boston. He went by way of Indianapolis, Indiana, Cincinnati, Ohio, and Roanoke and Daleville, Virginia, where he stopped to give addresses. From here he went to Norfolk, where he took a boat for Boston. At Norfolk he visited Ocean View, Fortress Monroe, Old Point Comfort, and Hampton Institute. He sailed on the *Juniata* past Portsmouth, which reminded him of the "Merrimac going out to seek its prey in March, 1863, and past Newport News the great ship building town, past the [site] of the Merrimac-Monitor fight, past Fort Monroe, across the Chesapeake. Between Capes Henry and Charles out on the great Atlantic."

Out on the ocean he wrote:

And this is out at sea—out on the great Atlantic. They say its a stormy pond, but it could hardly be more calm than this morning. Out on the bosom of the Infinite. How small and insignificant is man. How mighty is God who holdeth the oceans in the hollow of his hand—Save what may be in yonder small like craft not a sign of human life as far as one can see beyond the narrow confines of the Juniata. The sea, though ever in motion is this morning very even. Hardly as much stir made by it as by the constant thump of the great engines in the hold of the ship.

After some delays due to fogs, during which the boat lay at anchor, they arrived at Boston nearly twelve hours late. "The ride is monotonous. It would be much better with Mamma here. There is something that makes the sense of time almost vanish. I am ready to land whenever the ship is."

In all the unpublished writings of President Winger there is nothing more interesting and more revealing of the spirit of the man, of his interest in historic places, his ability to marshall literary and historical information to his use, and more revealing of the way he visited a city than his diary from July 1 to July 5 of 1922 on this visit to Boston. The diary for these days is therefore included just as recorded. In it is revealed a side of the man not known to people who met him at conferences or heard him in the pulpit.

July 1. And this is Boston. My first walk in the street leads me to Boston Commons. I came by the place last evening. Now another glimpse of it. Forty-eight acres in the very heart of this great city forever for the use of the common people. For all people, and they do use it. A great blessing to all.

Where shall I go first? Here is a party ready for Lexington and Concord. At once Barnes account of it —which I had almost committed when a boy—came back. The thought took possession of me and I join the party and we are off. We follow the guide. Here is the Arlington Church, where preached the great William Ellery Channing, the great Unitarian. Then down Commonwealth Avenue, due west from the Commons. It is the broadest and perhaps the wealthiest street in town, with its statues of great men. We cross Charles River on Mass. Avenue. Is that Harvard? Those grand buildings on the North Shore? No. Harvard has nothing so grand. They are the magnificent buildings of the Massachusetts Institute of Technology largely erected by Mr. Eastman of the Kodak Company. Later we pass through a part of Harvard's campus and on again.

We soon reach the point where Paul Revere in his ride entered this road. Then to Lexington, here and there, tablets explain, what happened here 147 years ago. We reach the village green—a picture of which I had carried from Barnes. Here is the statue of John Parker, who led the attack of Minute Men and who fell in the fight. Paul Revere had come down that road and awakened the entire countryside. They were aroused to defend their rights and their homes. Here in Lexington he had found John Hancock and Samuel Adams asleep and warned them. In this house we saw the bed in which they slept. Also the old drum beaten on this occasion. The house is still standing. The thought of that skirmish on the 19th of April, 1775 on the village green when the farmers met the British regulars under Pitcairn, 70 against 450, and though the patriots had to disperse, Lexington stands with Thermopylae. Here John Parker fell shot, bayoneted John Harrington, crawled across the road and died at his wife's feet. These spots seem sacred. We are off down the road which Paul Revere took toward Concord. About midway of the 14 miles from Lexington to Concord we pass the large rock marking place where Revere was taken prisoner that morning by British guards. He was taken back to Boston, though his partner escaped and aroused Concord.

As we drive into Concord—that wonderful literary center—still has that air—not so much touched by commercialism as some places most interesting places of later Revolutionary days are shown. To the right as we enter the town going Northwest—there lived Hawthorne—there Louisa May Alcott wrote Little Men. On the right lived Emerson for 40 years. Again, on the left lived Thoreau and further on, in the center of town the burial ground where all of these lie buried. The Wright Tavern is shown us where Major Pitcairn missed his Toddy and swore he would stir the blood of the damned Yankees before night. Turning to the right we almost seem to leave Concord. But this is not all. That old looking building on the left, showing that it had once been a fine one—is the Old Manse—Mosses from an Old Manse. Just past it the road turns again to the left, another view of it. And we approach a monument—An arched cement bridge—Concord Bridge.

> "By the rude bridge that arched the flood,
> Their flag to April's breeze unfurled,
> Here once the embattled farmers stood
> And fired the shot heard round the world."

To repicture the scene and the incidents that occurred here are too much. One can think—yes almost weep in the presence of such historic simplicity but grandeur. And we return. Another view of each of the famous homes. With a thought of the retreating British who more than found their match in that morning conflict. The past against the future.

We are again in Boston and now I try it myself— off for Harvard to Harvard Square. Not the great buildings of this great university. But where is Longfellow's home. Only a short distance. And on the way we pass the Chestnut tree where stood the village blacksmith. His old home—humble home made famous in that beautiful poem. And this is where Longfellow lived. The house that had been Washington's headquarters. Welcome. Saturday afternoon 3:00 p.m. This is his study. This his chair in which he sat and when tired of that there he stood and wrote—The most beloved of our *poets*. Here he died. And I thought as I looked at the famous picture

"With a glory of winter sunshine
Over his locks of gray
In the old historic mansion
He sat on his last birthday.
"With his books and pleasant pictures," etc.

Here again one thinks to deeply to express.

Only a short distance on lived his friend James Russell Lowell. In Lowell Mansion — there he was born —there he lived—there he died. On these grounds he played, where Lowell Drive now runs. I thought of some of his lines

"Thought of a mound in Mt. Auburn
Where a little headstone stood."

Yes, just across the street is that beautiful, wonderful cemetery, wonderful because here rests such as Longfellow, Lowell, Holmes and so many more—dozens of them famous in History. There on Indian Ridge is the tomb of Longfellow— his wife—his brother. not large —just a solid monument of granite. And down below— 20 feet lower—there is the grave of Lowell and his family—such a modest slab marking the site. And following this street further—the grave of Holmes.

Time fails for me to write my full impressions of these historic scenes. After this even Harvard's buildings were not full of surprises. That Institution, tho, nearly 300 years old, has so much of history. Here is the Washington Elm under which Washington took command. Here are the buildings in which so many great men taught and where many illustrious men were trained. Interesting.

Strange to my boys, but I didn't go "across the river" to see the Harvard Stadium, where occurs the football, baseball, etc. Where 50,000 people can behold.

After such a day amid historic scenes it is time to go home and rest and meditate.

Sunday, July 2—A Sunday in Boston.

A walk through the Boston Commons. That historic old place left an impression on me.

196

I attend church at Kings Chapel. The oldest church in Boston. It is Unitarian now. In the church yard at hand lies John Winthrop, John Endicott, and other notables.

In the afternoon a car ride showed us many places in Boston. The Bunker Hill Monument. The U. S. Navy Yard, where we went through the old frigate Constitution. Various other places of interest.

In the evening the song service at St. Paul's Chapel opposite the *Commons*. Tired, Letter writing. Retirement.

Monday, July 3.

A trip to Portland, Maine. Rain. Train leaves one hour later than I thought, so thru the rain, from North Side Station, I go to see the old North Meeting House, where were hung the lights to notify Paul Revere. How near to Boston lies the swamps and thickets. These we see as we hasten on. In Portland we stop an hour, visiting the birthplace of Henry W. Longfellow. Then on to New Brunswick, where Bowdoin College is located. The college of Longfellow, Hawthorne, Pierce and Peary. Here Longfellow's room is shown, and Peary's sled with which he reached the North Pole. After a busy day, we return to Boston again tired and weary.

July 4

Independence Day in Boston. The city is astir early. I am too. I walk various streets to see historic scenes. Franklin's birthplace near the Old South Meeting House, etc. But on State Street is the old state house, just in front of which occurred the Boston Massacre. As I stood here, on the very spot, I heard an Italian boy, the best student of Boston High School, read the Declaration of Independence in the presence of the Governor, etc.

Then to Faneuil Hall where the superintendent of Boston Schools gave an excellent address. In this hall, the cradle of Liberty, where had spoken James Otis, Samuel Adams, John Hancock, Daniel Webster, etc. A most impressive visit.

Then for a session of the N. E. A. in the Mechanics Hall. It was of little interest. Speeches were dry and could not be heard. I did not stay long until I went to Arlington Hotel to retire.

July 5

I took special note of some of the very fine churches. At Copley Square the Trinity Church, where Wendell Philipps spoke. The new Old South Meeting House, very fine, Boston Library and Boston University. On down ...... avenue passed Mechanics Hall is the Christian Science Church and publishing interests. These interested me far more than the N. E. A.

I left Boston before noon for New York, passing thru R. I. and Connecticut.

. . . . .

I have omitted my visit in the afternoon of July 4, to Plymouth. A fifty mile ride thru Mass. brings you to the landing of the Pilgrims. Quaint old town full of interest. The Plymouth Rock—Leyden Street, around the base of the hill, which had become the burial ground of half the number before the first winter had passed, the later cemetery on the hill where many lie buried, and on this hill stood the old fort. A very interesting city.

In the summer of 1926 President and Mrs. Winger and their son Paul visited the northeastern part of the United States. They went to Detroit, then eastward through Canada to Niagara, from there across New York State, "just missing Buffalo," visiting Ithaca, New York, the home of Cornell University, Syracuse University at Syracuse, New York, then down the St. Lawrence through the Adirondacks, across Lake Champlain by ferry into Vermont, through the Green Mountains, through the White Mountains of New Hampshire, then to Portland and Brunswick. From here they returned by way of Boston, New York, and Philadelphia, arriving home Saturday evening, July 31, having traveled two thousand nine hundred eighty miles.

The following are excerpts from notes of this trip:

July 19

The trip through Canada from Port Huron to Niagara, nearly two hundred miles was interesting. London was the chief city enroute, a good trade center and the location of the University of Western Ontario. Much of the land is not good for much but hay. The drive from Hamilton is through one rich garden and fruit orchard.

Niagara, the eternal thundering of waters, is ever grand. We had visited here on our wedding trip 24 years ago. It is as interesting as ever. We camped on the Canadian side, in sight of the Canadian Falls. The eternal mist, and the eternal pour and the eternal roar are all impressive. The view of the falls by night, as they are lighted up with powerful lights is beautiful.

July 22

The next day was spent among the Adirondacks. Most of this region is owned by the state of New York and has become the playground of the wealthy and those seeking rest. President Coolidge is spending his summer at a camp near Paul Smith's near Saranac Lake. We passed by the entrance to the summer White House grounds. Some beautiful mountain scenery may be seen on some of the main highways. The Ausable Chasm is well known. We camped that night at Plattsburg, on the back of the little bay where Captain McDonough so brilliantly defeated the British fleet in the war of 1812.

July 23

The next day we crossed Lake Champlain by ferry to Vermont. Lake Champlain is one of the most famous in our history. On its waters and on its banks have been fought many famous battles. Today it is a great highway of commerce, while its beautiful banks furnish summer homes for thousands of visitors. Vermont and the Green Mountains are as green and as beautiful as their names indicate. Many rich farms with large farm buildings were seen. One noted thing about the farm buildings of Vermont and other New England states is that the house and barn are joined together by a large woodshed, so that the farmer can go to his work without going out of doors. These people know how to keep their homes beautiful and clean.

There is yet enough of this day left for a drive through the White Mountains of New Hampshire. They are not as green nor as beautiful as the Green Mountains of Vermont. The point of most interest to us was the Old Man of the Mountains. Hawthorne has made this famous in his Great Stone Face. It takes no imagination to see that great cluster of rocks on the mountain side really does look like a man's face. It is very interesting. That night we camped in Crawford's notch near the foot of Mt. Washington, the highest mountain east of the Mississippi. The one thing to be remembered this night was the midges, a small sand fly that comes up to the camper in untold numbers. There was little sleep that night by any of the campers.

July 24

Portland is the metropolis of Maine. It is a great hustling city. We visited the home of Longfellow. We went thirty miles to the east to Brunswick, Me., the seat of Bowdoin College. We were interested much in this college, which while not so wealthy as others [has] produced some great men, such as, Longfellow, Hawthorne, Franklin Pierce, Robert M. Peary, T. B. Read, and Chief Justice Melville W. Fuller. Brunswick is famous as the place where Harriet Beecher Stowe wrote Uncle Toms Cabin. Brunswick was the eastern end of our journey and we turn our steps homeward.

July 25 to 27

North of Boston are the towns of Salem, Lexington, and Concord of much historic interest. Salem has been made famous by the Salem Witchcraft. The house is still shown where many of these unfortunate persons accused of witchcraft were accused. Salem has been made famous in literature by Hawthorne. Here is his birthplace. Here is the house where he moved when he was dismissed and where he wrote the Scarlet Letter. Here, too, is the House of Seven Gables. . . . But the older Salem is now largely occupied by a foreign people.

July 27

We leave Boston for a visit to places on south. We passed through Quincy, the home of the Adamses, presidents John and John Quincy. They are buried in the town church. Their homes are still standing. Plymouth is fifty miles southeast of Boston and has history as old as any other place in the United States save St. Augustine, Jamestown, New York and a few others. Here is Plymouth Rock on which the Pilgrims are said to have landed. Here many places are pointed out as the spots on which famous persons lived. The cemetery on burial hill contains the graves of some of the earliest settlers. The monument to the Pilgrim fathers is large and imposing. The monument to the Indians, Massasoit, is impressive. Plymouth impresses one as both ancient and modern. For in the midst of these historic scenes there is evidence on every hand of modern industry and business.

Visits to Brown University at Providence and Yale University at New Haven, Conn., completed our visit in New England. Both of these institutions are famous and interesting and have a long history.

The western visitor to New England notices the absence of much good farm land. Swamps, thickets and stone fields abound even in sight of Boston. New England on its scanty soil cannot compete in farming with rich lands farther west. They, however, made a record in manufacturing, building towns and homes, building schools and churches and have given to the country many of our greatest men and women.

July 28

We had the pleasure of the delightful drive from Tarrytown down the Hudson to New York. Tarrytown has been made famous by Washington Irving. Here is sleepy hollow bridge made famous in the story of Ichabod Crane. Near by is the cemetery where Washington is buried. In Tarrytown is the monument to Major Andre and the three patriots who captured him. As one goes down the river the palisades of the Hudson can be well seen on the opposite bank. We drove the entire length of Manhattan Island, through the busiest part of New York just to see the crowd and jam. There is really some kick in it. The ferry across the harbor, past the Statue of Liberty, is interesting. Another drive of 18 miles across Staten Island and a short ferry ride brings us to New Jersey. Seventy miles more through Princeton and Trenton brought us to Philadelphia.

Some of the preceding pages reveal President Winger's references to history and literature as he traveled. One can open his *Letters from Foreign Lands* or his diary and find his references to literature, history, or philosophy as he approached a historic spot. He was alive and alert in every fibre of his being. He was thoroughly extroverted and objective. He was awake, curious about everything that affects the life of people, or that has interested peoples in the past. That he lived intensely is shown by the fact that he would travel all day until late into the night and then return to his room and write his "Letters." These are really lengthy travelogs and are a testimony to both his energy and his intensely alert mind.

We include just a few paragraphs from his *Letters from Foreign Lands* as further evidence of the above observations:

Keilworth is a village that shows some age but there are many fine new English houses. We are not interested in the new houses but in the castle beyond. We walk the distance of less than a mile. The winding road leading to the castle is now a street with many new houses. We remember Scott's description of the great event when the Earl of Leicester gave the grand reception to Queen Elizabeth. Little Dickie Hobgoblin Flibbertigibbet with Wayland Smith and the unhappy army must have walked this unhappy road. We get our first sight of Keilworth Castle at the edge of a woods where the remains of an old wall may be seen. . . . The Earl of Leicester had a new roadway cut out through this part of the grounds and a bridge built across the moat.

Then when he got down to Italy, where centuries of ancient history had been enacted, history which he had taught us in college classes, he wrote:

Here is the Roman Forum. It is thrilling to stand here in the place that was once the center of the Roman World. Perhaps no other spot on earth has so much history crowded in such little space. The history of Rome for a thousand years centers here. It is a little valley of only a few acres between some of the hills of Rome. The Palatine Hill just described, is on the south. The Capitoline and Esquiline are on the north. At first this was the common meeting and trading place for the people centuries before Christ. Then they began making their laws here in the public meetings. Then they built temples to their pagan gods. Here arches were constructed to their conquering heroes. Here the mightiest of the Caesars erected temples and public buildings. But all is in ruins now as much as their palaces on yonder Palatine Hill.

Writing from Greece later, he said:

We are now within the walls of the Acropolis. We have a strange feeling as we view this famous precinct. For here was centered in a small space a thousand years of the history of a great people. Only two other places on earth have a history so intense—the Roman Forum and the Temple Site of Jerusalem. . . . The great rulers of Athens made its walls strong. Themistocles built this one on the north side and Cimon built the one on the south. To Themistocles and Pericles much of the credit is due for the grandeur of the place. Most of the work of Themistocles was destroyed but Pericles restored it on even a grander scale.

Here stood the ancient statue of Athena, built so high that with her glittering spear she could be seen far out at sea.

Halfway down the slope from the Acropolis is another hill not so famous in some respects but to us much more interesting. For this is Mar's Hill. . . . Here according to legend a tribunal of Athenians tried Mars for murder; hence the name. Here Socrates was tried and condemned to death. Just across the street is shown the prison where the famous philosopher spent his last days. But to us the event of most interest was that there Paul preached his great sermon found in Acts, seventeenth Chapter. We read it over again as we sit here. It is the best sermon we have heard today.

President Winger made a thorough survey of Jerusalem. He walked through its streets and its gates. He went around the city, outside its walls. As concluding paragraphs of his account of his visit to Jerusalem, he said:

Before leaving the city let us stand here for awhile and watch the crowd that is coming and going. Look at the people. Look at their animals and what they are doing. Here are high class Jews and Arabs wearing the red fez as a token of their station in life. Here is the Arab from the country, barefooted even in winter, though he may have a sandal held on by a strap between his toes. He usually has a striped dress but he always wears a kind of shawl around his head which he can wrap around his head and neck and tuck up under a band around his head. He always wears a heavy robe of some kind, both winter and summer; in winter to keep off the wind, and in summer to keep off the heat. Here is the peasant woman, shabbily dressed and as barefooted as her husband. If she is a good orthodox Moslem she will be dressed in black with a veil over her face. She is often carrying a heavy load on her head. It is remarkable what these poor people carry. . . . Here you will see the Russian Jew ecclesiastic, with full beard and a little curl hanging down the side of his temples so he can fulfill the admonition "not to mar the corners of his beard." Here are Greek, Latin, Armenian, Abyssinian, Coptic, and other priests of all orders and descriptions. As in the days of the apostles when there were in Jerusalem at Pentecost Parthians, Medes, Elamites, Dwellers in Mesopotamia, Judea, Cappadocia, Pontus, Asia, Phrygia, Pamphylia, Egypt, Libya, Cyprus, Rome, Jews, Proselytes, Cretes and Arabians—so today you will see at Jaffa Gate all these I have told you about and besides Arabs, Hindus, Negroes, Gypsies, Bedouins, beggars, ecclesiastics, business men, students, travellers, loafers, workers, guides, and mis-guided Russians, Poles, Germans, English, French, Austrians, Canadians, Americans, Christians, Jews, Mo-hammedans, and other folks, all sorts of men and women, in all sorts and conditions of clothing meet and jostle each other as they pass, or try to pass in this narrow thoroughfare.

You say you are confused. Well you have the right picture. That is just how it looks at Jaffa Gate at Jerusalem.

Another very revealing excerpt from his travel diary is this one describing the interesting experi-ence of taking a meal in a Bedouin home in Egypt:

We enter the village, a series of mud huts looking dirty enough. From what we can see we have stopped in the best home in town. Special preparations have been made to receive us. Here we are ready for our lunch which the guide has brought from the hotel, but the Arab woman is preparing coffee for us. We are sitting on an old sofa. An old rug has been spread for our feet. A small table has been placed before us. Water has been brought for washing our hands, a universal oriental custom. When the good woman of the house has spread the meal and brought the coffee, she and the guide retire and leave us alone to note more carefully the Arab home:

This is a fair sized room. The walls are of stone; the floor is of earth. Here is a box of bedding that is spread on the floor at night. Here are a few old pictures hung on the wall. Mrs. Winger does not care for her coffee but I save the reputation of the family by drinking both cups. Arab coffee is renowned you know, and it [would] be an insult not to drink it. We are invited to see the rest of the family. It would seem that three brothers live here with their families. A few such rooms as the one I have described enclose a kind of courtyard, in which the camels are fed, the geese [and] chickens are kept, the cats, the children and all the rest. Here in one room is a pile of shelled corn with a lot of eggs on top of the pile. Geese and chickens come in and help themselves. . . . We receive their God bless you and thank them for this rare privilege, mount our camels and ride away. We shall remember this as one of the unique experiences of the trip.

By the way of camel riding President Winger commented: "When the camel strikes a dromedary trot he does not ride so badly, but when he walks, ah me! Someone has said it is like riding an earthquake."

While in India he wrote:

I am going villaging with some of the native preachers. In a bullock cart that goes at the rapid rate of three miles an hour we go four or five miles to another village for a meeting. It is too dark to see the country and too jolty to sleep. When we arrive it is nearly ten and I am thinking that most of the folks must surely be in bed. We come to the house of Timothy, the native teacher and preacher. We are served tea and cakes. Native huts are all about and the place looks congested. One wonders how they keep fires from burning them out. Soon they start singing. And from many directions the people begin coming in. . . .

At another time, he wrote concerning a ride in a bullock cart: "Here is the hill down which D. L. Miller had a frightful ride behind a team of runaway bullocks. We wish our team were a little more frightened."

Here are some fine-looking women dressed fairly well. Here are some scarcely dressed at all. On some of the women we count forty and fifty rings hanging to wrists, ankles, noses, foreheads, and ears. Some women look haggard and some look happy. Here are Indian men, some who look refined and some who look like savages. Here is one who calls himself a holy man. He is dressed like a woman but is as dirty as a pig. He has paid nothing for a ticket, and when asked how he can travel that way he says he has a pass from Almighty God. When he asks for money he is told to get that where he gets his railroad pass. It is interesting and instructive to ride third class with this motley crowd. The missionaries have their bedding roll which they spread down for cushions, and also for sanitary reasons. They carry their drinking water, too, though at every station we can buy tangerines that are juicy and safe to use.

[March 20 and 21, 1928.] Ira [Moomaw] and I

207

visit a rich Hindu farmer. Eat with him at his home in Anklesvar and visit his fields at edge of city. With I. S. Long I visit rich Mohammedans and drink tea with them. Here we saw the greatest display of monkeys. Monkeys carrying their baby monkeys. We also visit wealthy Parsees. Cotton gins and a silk mill. We visit a village school nearby. Eat in wealthy Christian's home and at poorer Christian's home.

His Writings and Other Interests

President Winger's writings were more or less incidental to the great work he did as a college president and a churchman. Anyone observing his work as a college president or as a churchman would scarcely realize that he was at the same time in the process of writing a manuscript. In fact, on the surface it was difficult to see when he wrote his books. His diaries do not contain many references to his manuscripts. He said very little to his associates at the college about the books he was writing. Only occasionally would he say in his diary that he had worked on his book or had gone to see the printer about his book.

But he was a much more systematic worker than appeared to a casual observer. For many years he himself kept up at the college long mailing lists of prospective students and prospective donors. He worked at this persistently and systematically. It must have taken years of systematic work to collect the original data on which he based his *History of the Church of the Brethren in Indiana.* For a quarter of a century or more he kept up a daily diary.

One begins to understand when he wrote his books when his sons testify that, while they were living at home, scarcely ever did they find their father in bed when they arrived home.

He was in his college office writing letters—or at least writing. He usually wrote letters or prepared talks for an hour or two before breakfast. It was a rare occasion when any member of the family came down in the morning without finding Father at work or taking a quick walk around the college campus. Six hours seemed all he could spare for sleep and he was a bit impatient of others who would sleep seven or eight.

Early in 1936, on a trip to California, where he gave more than twenty addresses in seven days, he had a typewriter with him; he said, ". . . spent the day in club car on my typewriter," on both the way out and the way back. Immediately on his return he went to see a printer about his book. At many board meetings and conferences he took his work with him and spent time in his hotel or in a library at work. In their travels he would no more get to an important library where he could find materials he wanted than he was in it at work. This ability to segregate a task and carry it along with other work was phenomenal. The ability to tear away from certain other duties and pursue a purpose such as writing one of his books was marvelous. The drive and energy he put into the pursuit of his ends marked him off from the average man.

His books were written for the popular reader, for the average man who was not so much interested in erudition as in general information. He wrote in good Anglo-Saxon language in an easy-flowing style. His later works are better than his earlier ones. Thirty years of writing for all sorts of purposes brought about a progressive refinement and general improvement in his writing.

He spent many years of research at odd and unusual hours and places to collect data, especially for his Indian books, but also for his *Life of Elder R. H. Miller* and his history books. These works are not without errors in fact, due, no doubt, to his writing "on the run," but even then he collected much valuable and dependable information that had never been brought together.

In his *Memories of Manchester* he says, "Church History has always been a favorite study of mine. The Church of the Brethren has had its share of strong men and interesting history. I like to write books." It is not strange then that his first book should have been the biography of one of the strong men of the church, Elder Robert Henry Miller.

This first book was published in 1910. Elder Miller, whom President Winger refers to as "Brother Robert" throughout the book, was a self-made man of unusual gifts who largely through private study made of himself a great Bible student and preacher. He first came to prominence in the District of Southern Indiana, near Ladoga, and then came to be a nationally known debater, preacher, college president, and church statesman of the first order. His last decade was spent as pastor of the Church of the Brethren at North Manchester, Indiana. He died in 1892 at Mount Morris, Illinois, where he had gone to deliver a series of Bible lectures.

President Winger's book shows great admiration for Brother Robert, tells the story of his life, shows how he came to prominence, and recounts his great work in public debates and in church affairs. The book contains a splendid account of the way both the "Old Orders" and the "Progressive Brethren" broke from the Church of the Brethren in 1881 and 1882 respectively. There is also a collection of excellent brief biographies of R. H. Miller's contemporaries, such as John Kline, George Wolfe, Henry Kurtz, James Quinter, D. P. Saylor, Enoch Eby, and Daniel Vaniman. The book contains samples of R. H. Miller's "editorials" and his sermons. It is a useful book and contains much valuable material, though the style of writing is not in Otho Winger's best.

His second book was *History of the Church of the Brethren in Indiana,* published in 1917. This book contains a brief sketch of one hundred twenty-five congregations within the state and of the many leaders of the past and at the time of writing. It also contains a fifty-page history of Manchester College.

The book is a useful beginning of Indiana Brethren history. While there are many minor errors in it on matters of detail, in the main it is a dependable record and represents much valuable information. It seems almost impossible that a man as busy as President Winger was in college and church affairs at this time could collect from over the state so much material. At this writing (1951) the book is being rewritten and brought down to date.

In 1919 he published his third book, *The History and Doctrines of the Church of the Brethren.* He says, in the preface, that this book grew out of "the felt need of a book for my classes dealing with the Church of the Brethren." The early history of the church in Europe and its earliest days in America had been written by Dr. M. G. Brumbaugh. Other aspects of our church history have been told by other later authors. This book was written for "the student or reader who desires a general and connected view."

This book is an outline history of the church, containing chapters on our origins in Europe, the establishing of the church in America, the colonial church, its expansion and growth, dissension and division within the church, the history of missions and education within the church, church publications, Sunday schools, Annual Meetings, church polity, Christian life and worship, church doctrine and ordinances, and some biographies of leaders.

It is largely written from secondary sources, and, while providing a general connected story of the history of the church, does not represent the original research of his Indiana history. The book makes frequent use of extended quotations from the works of others. It would seem that this book could be made the outline upon which his students could at some time base extensive research in the history of the Brethren. As it is, it is a useful book for the general reader.

In 1928 Otho Winger published his *Letters from Foreign Lands*. This is the story of his trip around the world. It is a travelog, but it is more. There is much historical material in it, as well as many literary references and observations of a philosophic and religious nature.

His comments at historic spots such as Schwarzenau, Rome, Athens, and Jerusalem are rich in historic information and make intensely interesting reading, revealing both his historical knowledge and the depth and aspirations of his own life. The book is a monument to his boundless energy. It was largely written while enroute.

In 1940 he published *Memories of Manchester,* the story of his connection with Manchester College. It tells the story of his student days, his teaching days, and his years as president of the college. In his own words it tells the story of interesting aspects of building the college. The book contains a select number of his chapel talks and interesting anecdotes that occurred at the college. It is well written and intensely interesting, especially to students and faculty members who know Manchester, and was evidently largely written from memory. Its informal style and intensely human aspects make it a delightful book to read, both for information about the college and about Otho Winger.

President Winger wrote several books on Indian life between 1933 and 1936. They were *The Frances Slocum Trail; "The Kenopocomoco," Eel River, the Home of Little Turtle; The Last of the Miamis;* and *The Lost Sister Among the Miamis.* Something more about the Indian books will be told on other pages.

The last of his booklets was a pamphlet published in 1944, *In Memory of Ida Miller Winger,* a tender retelling of the years he and Mrs. Winger spent together, with emphasis on their travels and the story of her death and burial.

Otho Winger's reputation does not rest chiefly on his books, but they added to his stature in the eyes of the public. That he could discipline himself to write books at the same time that he was carrying on a multifarious list of other activities is an evidence of his strength of will and of the diversity of his abilities. It might well prove that his Indian stories would be the most lasting of his writings. There come to the desk of the president of Manchester College now frequent requests for copies of these Indian books.

Other Interests

President Winger made his major contribution to society in the fields of education and religion. He served church and school and related institutions throughout life. He never sought public office for himself, nor did he take an active part in politics. Members of his staff sought public office and participated in political affairs with his consent and encouragement. He was, however, a keen observer of political movements and would likely have been successful in the field of politics had he chosen to enter it.

There were, however, several lines of public activity in which he had an interest and in which he participated. The American Friends Service Committee was putting on a state-wide campaign for Russian relief in 1922. They wanted big men for sponsors, and asked President Winger to act as one of them. He accepted and arranged certain meetings at North Manchester and elsewhere in Wabash County. Another of these interests was public highways. In 1931 and 1932, some of the people in North Manchester took an active interest in public highways. President Winger records having made several trips to Indianapolis with local politicians in the interest of better roads and refers to some lobbying experience in the state senate. On another occasion he attended a meeting at Huntington in the interest of the same cause.

In the mid-thirties there was a movement on in Indiana to tax some heretofore-untaxed properties held by colleges, churches, and lodges. President Winger became quite interested in helping the colleges retain their tax-exempt status in relation to these properties. Those interested in seeing that all taxable property not rightly exempt should bear its share of the tax load pressed their case in the legislature. The colleges and other organizations attempted to protect their interests. John Atherton, treasurer of Butler University, who was a member of the senate, also represented the church-related and independent colleges on the legislative committee of their association, and was very active in the interest of the colleges. He reported that President Winger did very effective work in northern Indiana by contacting many alumni and friends in various counties in person, thus bringing pressure on legislators who would decide the issue. He also wrote to state senators and representatives making his appeal for the colleges. The issue was finally compromised. After a given date colleges were to pay tax on all income-producing properties not actually in use for college purposes.

After the legislature was closed, Dr. Winger wrote to Governor Clifford Townshend saying:

I want to express my appreciation both to the legislature and to you for the settlement made about the

1933 ...

1934 ...

1935 ...

1936 ...

1937 ...

Photostatic Pages of His Diary for 1933-1937

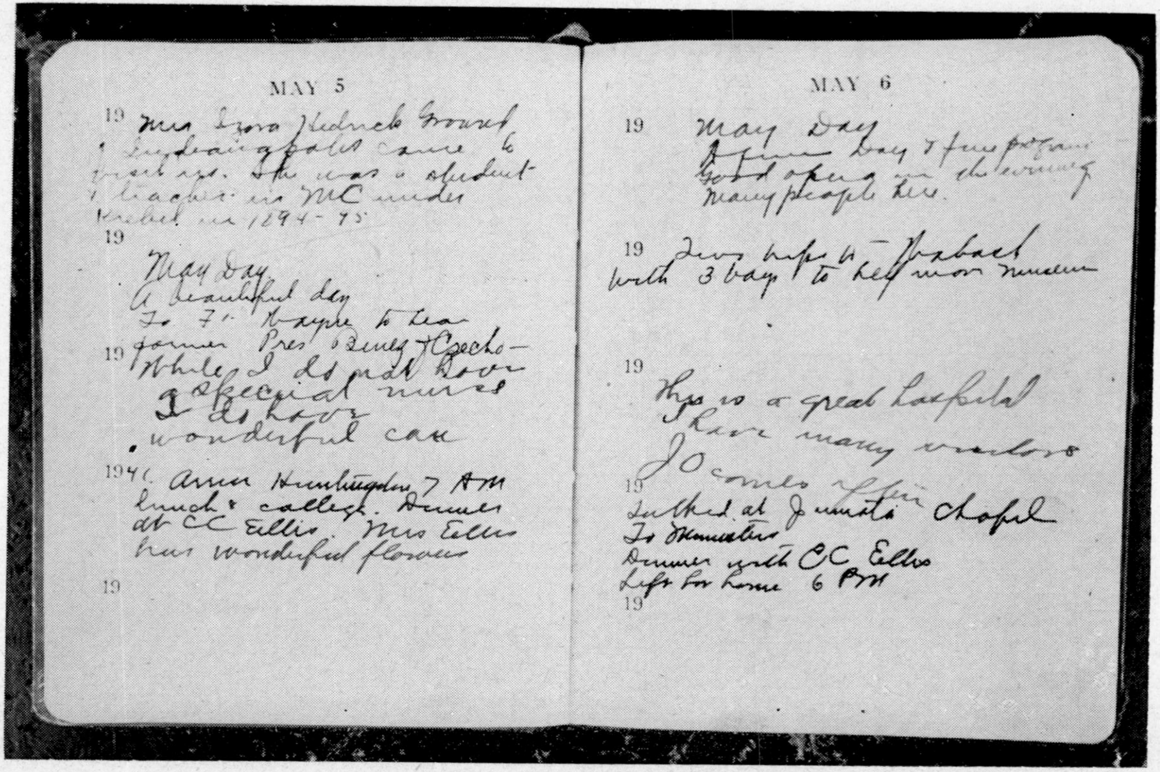

Photostatic Pages of His Diary for 1938-1942

taxation of colleges. I am perfectly agreed that income producing real estate, other than that used for college purposes should be put on the tax duplicates. I think the settlement was a fair one, and I want to assure you that we college folk appreciated it very much.

President Winger had a keen interest in local history of all kinds. He was an active member of the Wabash County Historical Society and helped publish a history of the county. He encouraged the establishment of local historical societies in other surrounding cities, such as Columbia City and Marion, giving practical advice on how to go about developing such a society.

An example of his influence in this field is a letter from Dick Simmons, of Marion, dated September 3, 1938:

Words are inadequate to express my gratitude for the many fine things you have done for me and for the History Club during the past two and a half years. . . . It was the talk that you gave before the student body of Marion High School in March, 1936, that aroused the enthusiasm necessary to start our organization and since that time the help that you have so unselfishly given has enabled our organization to advance. . . . Your help in our attempt to organize a State Junior Historial Society has been invaluable.

President Winger was a friend of Ross Lockridge of Indiana University, who was a specialist in Indiana local history, and they often worked together on projects.

As a result of this interest and activity he was notified on May 14, 1941, that he had been elected an honorary member of the Indiana Historical Society.

Honorary membership is conferred by action of the committee; it is limited among other respects to those who have rendered exceptional service to the Society and to the cause of history in the state. You are therefore, henceforth, an honored member of the Society exempt from the payment of dues.—Christopher B. Coleman, Secretary.

He had another interest which he promoted assiduously all through the middle and late thirties. It is quite difficult to get a clear picture of what all he was doing. But among other things he wanted the Frances Slocum Trail between Peru and Marion properly marked, to have some suitable monument placed at the spot where the Battle of the Mississinewa was fought, and to have parks established along the Frances Slocum Trail.

To achieve these ends he used his influence on the Conservation Department of the state, the State Highway Department, and perhaps the State Historical Society. He spoke to the luncheon clubs in Peru, Wabash, and Marion about these matters. He addressed a combined meeting of Kiwanians of the three cities. He had a board of directors appointed to promote the park movement and was appointed its chairman. The state agreed to pay twenty-five dollars per acre for park lands. Committees were appointed in each of the three cities to negotiate for the land, and to raise additional funds to supplement the money secured from the state. To promote this project he wrote many letters, made numerous trips all around the route, gave many speeches, and did everything else he could.

At one time in 1937, with the help of some

Indians and college students, he put on a pageant at Wabash re-enacting some early Indian history, in order to promote interest in this movement. He wrote a booklet called *The Frances Slocum Trail,* describing the scenes along the trail and the history that had been enacted there. He also prepared a map of the Frances Slocum Trail which was published in a number of the newspapers of the state. In 1938 he attended a celebration of the Mississinewa Park victory at Peru.

In a letter to H. C. Early in 1937 he referred to his interest in working with a group of businessmen of three or four counties on this public project, "finding locations for new parks, putting up historical signs and so forth," and expressed his keen interest in it. In this he found recreation from his duties at the college. In private correspondence he told of the relaxation he found in tramping over the old Indian trails picking up a bit of lore here and there.

To a friend he wrote in September of 1936:

I am taking it a little easy since school opened. I am spending [a] little time on my hobby. I spent yesterday climbing banks and hopping ditches, walking through woods and snapping pictures along the Mississinewa. I am going back today. I am interested in it and find it a wonderful relief. I never slept better in my life than last night.

President Winger's diary is full of references to the events in Europe and Asia—the war between China and Japan, the war in Spain, Italy's attack on Albania, Hitler's persecution of the Jews, the swallowing of Czechoslovakia and Austria, Chamberlain's visit to Hitler, the meeting of Hitler and Mussolini in Rome, and war in Poland, Norway, and France. These are interspersed with forebodings and laments at the trends world affairs had taken. He was aware of what was happening and had some appreciation of the significance of it. "Are we drifting into another World War?" he asked.

In his diary are also found references to election results, the deaths of "Teddy" Roosevelt and Woodrow Wilson, the defeat of Charles Hughes, the sickness and death of Howard Taft, the death of Knute Rockne, and many, many other references to matters of general public interest.

President Winger grew up in a community near an Indian reservation. From 1895 to 1898, he taught school in Indian Village, where many of his students were Indians. He always had an interest in these Indians, but that interest lay dormant for many years. In later years, when wrestling with college problems became routine and perhaps tiresome, as a matter of recreation he became actively interested in Indian history and spent much time, money, and energy in pursuing this hobby.

The degree of his absorption in this Indian hobby is almost unbelievable. It led him to the libraries in great centers like Chicago, Philadelphia, and Washington to do research. It led him to bookstores, especially second-hand bookstores, where he bought rare and expensive books on the Indians. He collected an unusually fine library of Indian books. It led him to Indian homes where he spent hours talking with the older Indians who knew Indian lore. He drove hundreds of miles as far west as Kansas and Oklahoma in search of Indian history.

This consuming interest was an avocation, a recreation from his pressing duties at the college. Through this interest he made new contacts with other people and with new subjects of study.

Since this interest developed largely during the author's sojourn in Kansas, he has asked President Winger's son, Paul, who has continued the study and has much of his father's Indian library, to write an account of Dr. Winger's Indian studies. He has written the following section, which, because of its intense interest, seems all too brief.

Father's Interest in Indians
by Paul M. Winger

As far back as I can remember Father was interested in Indian history. I believe that this interest can be attributed to three things. The old Winger homestead in Grant County was located close to the last Indian reservation in Indiana. As a young man, Father learned to know the descendants of such Indian greats as Little Turtle, Chief Godfroy, and Frances Slocum. He was stirred by the stories these people could tell him. In later years it was a cause of great regret with him that he had not taken notes in these visits with those with whom he came into contact.

A second cause for his interest in the Indians was his love of history. As a college professor he taught in several subject fields, but outside of philosophy his greatest love was probably that of history. His memory was prodigious and he could recite from memory most of the important dates of history. It was always a source of amazement to me that with all his other duties Father could discuss almost any phase of history. He enjoyed digging up new facts about early history, especially as it pertained to pioneer days in Indiana and the Indians who lived here. He visited most of the county libraries in northern Indiana and spent hours in reviewing land abstracts that would give him a clue to some family of interest.

A third reason for this interest in Indians stemmed from his humanitarian feelings for a great race of people. As he came to know and understand Indian history, he felt a great sorrow that such a race of people had been reduced in a few generations from the sole ownership of all the land in the Midwest to a position of being virtually "wards of the state."

In the early part of the nineteenth century the land in Indiana was gradually taken over by the white man. A history of the period would show the numerous treaties between the United States government and the Indian chiefs. The Indians who lived in this great state were either taken by the government to Kansas and Oklahoma or were confined to a relatively small area. The last such reservation in the state was along the Mississinewa River. This was only six miles from the old Winger homestead.

In 1896, Father graduated from the eighth grade. He was much interested in going on to college. Family finances made this impossible and in

August of that year Father took the county teacher examination. He was one of fourteen applicants who were assigned schools. He was given the Indian school north and east of Jalapa. This school was some six miles from home and for most of the year he walked or rode horseback. I can remember hearing Grandmother Winger tell of the times when he arrived home some bitter cold nights with fingers and toes half frozen. Father taught in this school for three years and came to know the families of the children he had in school. Here he was in the very heart of the land that had seen fighting between William Henry Harrison and the Indians in 1812. Here were relatives of Frances Slocum and Little Turtle. These stories thrilled him and were forever a source of interest. Father taught in this Indian school from 1895 to 1898.

A picture of the school taken in 1896 shows thirty-four students. While teaching here Father once stayed all night with William Piconga. William was a grandson of Chief Meshingomesia and his wife was a granddaughter of Frances Slocum. During this time, he came to know other relatives and friends of Chief Godfroy, Little Turtle, LaFount, and the Slocums.

During the twenty-five years of college attendance, public school work, and early years as a college president, Father simply did not have the time to devote to this hobby. He retained his interest and I am sure his determination was to put in writing some day some of the stories of the Indians that he had heard as a boy.

When college duties became severe, he would

hop in the car and go to visit the sites of which he later wrote. I can remember many Sunday afternoons when he would drive down to Grant County and renew old acquaintances. I know that he took notes on these occasions with the obvious intent of using them later on. He never went without his camera and he snapped literally thousands of pictures.

The many years of work finally culminated in 1933 when Father published a booklet entitled *The Frances Slocum Trail*. Most of the stories he heard in childhood were included in this book. This was revised and enlarged in 1943. In this later edition were included some one hundred twenty pictures. In all his writings concerning the Mississinewa, Father was grateful for the interest and assistance given by the Honorable Hal Phelps, judge of the Miami County circuit court.

In 1934, the year following the publication of *The Frances Slocum Trail*, Father published a second booklet entitled *"The Kenopocomoco," Eel River, the Home of Little Turtle*. This booklet describes Eel River and the Indians who lived there. Much of this was difficult material and had to be dug out of early county histories and compiled into readable material. Charles More from Fort Wayne was a student of Little Turtle. Father and Mr. More compared notes frequently. I believe Father personally visited every place mentioned in his first two booklets.

In 1935 came the third in the series of booklets dealing with the Indians. Father had become a great admirer of the Miami Indians. In this latest book,

The Last of the Miamis, he attempted to trace the history of this great Indian nation. This booklet also traced most of the Miami families who had been permitted to remain.

For many years Father had been intrigued with the story of Frances Slocum. He had visited her old home in Pennsylvania and had wanted to write this amazing story. In 1936 he published *The Lost Sister Among the Miamis.* This was a story, told in a very simple way, of this Pennsylvania girl who was stolen by the Indians and who lived with them for sixty years before she was found by her family. This book has had an excellent reception and can be found in most libraries in northern Indiana.

For thirty years Father had traveled extensively all over northern Indiana. He had written of the Miamis who had lived along the Eel, Wabash, and Mississinewa rivers and of their first cousins, the Potowatomi, who lived in northern Indiana and southern Michigan.

During the years 1936-1938, Father made many trips to find what he could about these Potowatomi Indians. He even made one trip to Oklahoma to find some descendants. The book, *The Potowatomi Indians,* was published in 1939. This was in many respects the best of Father's Indian books. It contains many of the thrilling stories of early conflicts with the Potowatomi Indians.

Few men have had private libraries on the Indian as extensive as the one Father gathered. I know that if health had permitted he would have had some further publications.

Father did not find relaxation in the average

way. He often remarked that his interest in Indians was his golf and his fishing. He spent much time, energy, and money on his hobby. During the last fifteen years of his life few things gave him as much pleasure. I am glad he left to us some of this Indian history that otherwise would never have been written.

His Devotion to His Family

Otho Winger was greatly devoted to his family. We have seen that as a boy, the oldest son in the family, he helped his mother care for the younger children, and seemed to assume an unusual responsibility for them.

He seemed much devoted to the old home community, and the old Cart Creek church; to it he returned again and again throughout his life to preach at regular or special sessions, to preach the funerals of old neighbors and friends, and to attend family reunions or community reunions. In his diary of July 6, 1924, he says, "Went to Cart Creek, Mt. 16:18. Lived again amid the scenes of my childhood."

When his parents were aging they moved, doubtless through his influence, to the same block in which he lived, just around the corner from his home in North Manchester. It was a simple frame home only a half block from the college. He visited there often and at all hours, took them with him to meetings and to funerals, and in their sickness was most attentive to their needs. Notes like these appear in his diary frequently. April 27, 1922: "Commencement at Banquo. Father and Mother went with me."

His father died on June 5, 1922, after a brief

illness. During the days of his illness Otho's diary is filled with brief references to his father's condition. On May 7 he says, "He has been suffering and is weakening faster than we know. Could we only have realized—well, what could we have done? Life is a brief busy span of time." On May 17: "C. M. Wenger went over and talked with Father Winger, who was most too weak to talk, but who enjoyed it very much. Two Wingers very much alike." On May 29 to June 3: "Father was not well. Almost paralyzed." June 4: "Father in great pain." And on June 5, after describing his condition, he says, "Nothing could be done. He passed away at 9:30. Gone." On the next day he says, "Many visitors come. Children all there. Again and again we go to the room. He looks like father asleep. But, he is not there. Only his form. No response to our sorrow and tears." The funeral was on the seventh at the Walnut Street church and burial was made in the Mt. Vernon cemetery. "A large crowd there. Last view and farewell to father. 'Till we meet again.' "

His mother lived on in the old home until 1933. She suffered frequent illnesses during this time and Otho and the family cared for her in a remarkable way.

President Winger, in an article written for publication at the time of his mother's death, said:

Her life is but representative of other good Christian mothers and we hope this appreciation will be a tribute to them also and encourage others to live well.

Mother's life was one of hard work. As a member of a large family, at an early age she had to quit school to help earn means for the family. After marriage she

assumed an unusually large part of the work with father.
. . . Besides the many duties at home, she found time
to be present to help wherever sickness or death were
found in the community.

Next to her family or even on a par with them
she found her greatest joy in the work of the church.
She was loyal to her church and its principles and sel-
dom found time or cause to complain or criticize. All
of her children and grandchildren have united with the
church as soon as they were old enough. Two of her
sons and two sons-in-law are ministers in the church
and her youngest daughter, Mabel, is a missionary. Her
gifts to the church were limited only by her ability to
give.

Mother had very few educational advantages, but
few people have been more interested in helping others
to an education. She sacrificed that all seven of her
children might go to college. . . . Some of their last plans
together were that a large part of their material means
should go to the college. Nothing gave her more joy in
her last days than the daily music of the college chimes.
. . . She gave freely to this cause [missions] and her
greatest sacrifice was when she gave Mable for the Mission
work of the church—knowing her age and the nature of
her disease she almost certainly knew that they would
never meet again in this world. But her faith and hope
never failed her that they would meet in our heavenly
Father's home.

A picture of the family group is shown in his
diary for January 19, 1923.

Mabel's last day with us. We eat supper at Mother's.
Spend the evening at our home. All the children home
but Eds. Also A. W. Ross and R. H. Miller. A session
of prayer and meditation. Mabel and Ira leave for India.
. . . It is a new experience to give a sister to go so far
from home with but little prospect of seeing Mother again.

And on January 24, 1930, his diary reads, "I

go to Warsaw to get the Moomaw's coming from India. Mabel and Ira have been gone seven years and bring back two fine boys, David and Richard. All glad to see them." It is a joy to record that Mother Winger was still living when Mabel first returned from the field.

There is every evidence that Otho Winger had an affectionate regard for his brothers and sisters, and that it was not merely a sentimental thing, for it bore fruit in genuine concern for their welfare, and in service and sacrifice for them.

Sister Cora lived nextdoor to Otho. Her husband, Lawrence Shultz, was the librarian at the college for many years. Otho was most helpful to her family, especially in times of sickness. His sister, Ethel, was employed at the college cooking establishment in his later years. The home of his oldest sister, Lizzie, was in North Manchester and he often called upon them and sometimes they accompanied him to his preaching appointments. John, his youngest brother, was a farmer with a large family living near North Manchester. Otho took great interest in him and his family and was most helpful to him and helped his family in many ways. John's daughter, Irene, was her uncle's very accomplished secretary for a time. Mabel was his youngest sister; after spending many years in the India mission field, the Moomaws returned because of ill-health and now live in New Jersey; he is employed in the New York offices of Agricultural Missions, Inc.

There are many references in his diary of thoughtful and kindly concern for his wife. His own pamphlet in honor of Ida tells the story beautifully.

In other sections of this book we have referred to their relationship. Suffice it to say here that many of Mrs. Winger's letters to Otho tell of her suffering due to her hip trouble, and his letters to her express his concern for her. Her concern for his health in turn was abundantly evident. That he sustained a deep, tender love and affection for her is evidenced in many ways. Their life together was an enriching fellowship for nearly forty-two years.

President Winger's interest in their two boys, Robert and Paul, was manifested in his letters. An occasional reference to them appears in his diary. Once he writes, "Went fishing with Paul, (Galen Kintner fell in)." Another time: "Work in the office, hickory nut hunting in the P.M." In one of his daily diaries we find, "Mamma is not feeling well, Paul is hoarse. Robert cut a big gash in his head. Papa is worn out." This must have been written in the same mood he was in the day he wrote of an institute held at Troy, Ohio: "Crowd small, roads bad, three lectures—God—Man—Sin."

Paul writes: "When we were small he used to take us swimming. It was quite an occasion to jump into the old Ford and drive to one of the neighboring lakes for a swim. In his younger days, Father had been an excellent swimmer and he wanted both his boys to learn." He also reports that his "father carried this game (idea) to our table and we often had guessing games on history and literature at the table."

While Mrs. Winger was in Chicago during 1913 and the boys were at home with their father his letters had much to say about the boys. During his high school days and through his college career, Paul was a member of a very successful basketball team. A few of the boys who were good players from the North Manchester high school came directly to college and continued playing together. The notes in his diary record the scores made in many of these games, newspaper comments about their playing, and a father's pardonable pride in his son.

When President and Mrs. Winger started on their trip around the world Paul took them to Fort Wayne and watched the train pull out for New York. The Wingers both found it very difficult to go, leaving him standing there alone. When they returned the next June, Paul went to California to meet them at the boat; they tell how their hearts were gladdened. President Winger's letters to the boys, which were frequent, his notes in his diaries, and his remarks to his friends indicated how he followed their careers and how concerned he was that they make good in their professions; and when they did succeed and received promotions he was highly pleased.

In his later years he sometimes expressed a regret that neither of his sons had taken up the ministry, but he rejoiced in their successes in educational work. Since his death, both boys have received promotions that would have made his heart glad. Robert is now assistant director of vocational education in the State of Michigan and Paul has recently become the superintendent of schools of Niles, Michigan. One feels certain that further promotions await them. Robert married

Otho Winger in His Late Fifties

President and Mrs. Winger With Their Sons, Paul and Robert

The Wingers, Their Sons, Daughters-in-law, and Grandchildren at Christmas

Lucile Eberwine of near Pitsburg, Ohio, and they have two daughters, Vivian and Reva. Paul married Esther Dohner of West Milton, Ohio. Their children are Joe and Louann.

In the thirties, President and Mrs. Winger made frequent trips to visit the boys. Paul was in school work, first as a principal of schools, and then as the superintendent at Sturgis, Michigan. Robert had long been teaching in the Detroit high schools. Often their father had a preaching or lecture engagement along the way or in Detroit. On going to Detroit or on their returning, or both, they would stop at Sturgis, thus visiting both of the boys and having some time for the grandchildren.

The boys report that after they left home they could always count on two or three letters a week from their father. He was always keenly interested but especially so in time of sickness, when his letters and telephone calls were even more frequent. These letters varied in length, usually very short in late years, but some running into many pages. They were written late at night, or early in the morning. Members of the family testify that after his death, when the letters ceased, they "felt very keenly the loss of contact, through these letters."

Like most grandfathers, President Winger took great pride in his grandchildren. On December 30, 1922, he recorded in his diary: "A great day. I went to Wabash, Mother to Marion, Robert drives through from Ohio, Lucile and Vivian come by train, a granddaughter in the home." On his birthday in 1923 he wrote:

Let me record a few things on these pages concerning Vivian. She is not yet a year old, but she has come to fill a large place in our lives and thought. She has been developing day by day into a beautiful, lively interesting child,—what hopes and possibilities are wrapped up within her life; we shall watch and aid in every way while she developes. They say she looks like her Grandpa, but he thinks she is the image of her mother. The truth is I guess she looks like her father and mother.

On September 22, 1924, he wrote: "These are days when Vivian is developing rapidly. Says so many new things. Thinks of so many new things. Remembers so well." On February 6, 1925, he said, "Somewhere in these notes we must not forget to note the rapid development of our little girl. At twenty-six months she tries to say everything—she uses nouns and adjectives freely but not prepositions and pronouns—she likes candy too well. She is attracting much attention."

In March of 1930 while in Detroit he says, "Vivian has the measles. Reva is lively." In November while the Wingers were on a visit to Robert's home in Detroit again, Robert, Ida, and Edith made a trip to Canada and "I spent the day with the children." And again on December 29, at home: "A day off to play with the grandchildren." These are among his few references to play.

When Joe D. was born he was quite frail. On April 10, 1935, Otho recorded this: "Paul is 28 today. I sent him flowers. Little Joe D. is sick. We are quite anxious about him." On the 25th: "Joe D. Hospital Kal. [Kalamazoo] operation may have to have another." And on the 28th: "In the afternoon to Sturgis, Little Joe D. has a major operation. Only four weeks old—6 pounds." But Joe D. recovered and grew. On March 4, 1939, he wrote: "Joe is 4 today. Louann is growing." And on June 30, 1939, he said, "Paul's here—Louann is some girl and Joe is some boy." All these indicate a constant interest in all four of his grandchildren, Vivian, Reva, Joe D., and Louann.

When Vivian began to teach school at Pitsburg, Ohio, she made her home with her grandparents, the Eberwines. In the last few years of his life, her Grandfather Winger wrote to her frequently; in fact, in one of the files the author found more than fifty letters and cards from 1943 to 1945. They were short messages of appreciation and keen grandfatherly solicitude. They often sound more like a father's letters to a daughter in whom he had a deep concern. These excerpts indicate in general their nature:

Yes Vivian we love you very much. We are proud of you and hope to see you grow into a strong, wise, good woman. We send you much love, sister, Daddy and Mother. . . . It may be that you will have the experience that many beginning teachers have had—an evening or two of discouragement, almost feeling you would like to quit, but get a good night of sleep and you will be better. You have almost everything in your favor for success and we know you will. When you write, tell us how you spent last Sunday. . . . The biggest thing for your success is to use good common sense, all that you can command. Be courteous to others, your superintendent and fellow teachers. Love your kiddies even if some are aggravating. Of course, you will keep order but do it through skill and tact. We hope you will get right into church and Sunday School.

The following entire letter is included because it is characteristic of all his letters.

Maple Oaks, Wednesday Morning
January 17, 1944

Dear Vivian:

The mailman just went and left us your letter. And we are most happy to receive it and read it twice. It sounds very good to us. It sounds like you are making good, and that is what we want to hear. Tell Grandma E. we are anxious to hear from her about the work of her granddaughter; ours too. Grandma W. has some pain this week, but Edith is taking good care of her. Edith is also doing some canning for the McMullens, who are so sick and needy.

Your letter sounds like you must be doing good work with your kiddies. Of course, we knew that you would; only we were just anxious to hear. Keep the good work going. It is fine you can do some work for the grandpa's. And with your hard work you will need plenty of sleep. In your next letter tell us something about church and Sunday School.

It's fine that you are beginning to get checks of your own. We know that you will be careful how you spend it, so you will have a good balance when school closes next spring. How is your car acting and costing?

Did I tell you that Frances Slocum, Jr., is coming from Pennsylvania to Indiana next week. I am to attend some meetings that are being arranged for her. Our District Meeting will be here in Manchester next week.

Again we thank you for your very good letter. We know you are busy, but when you find time to write us a line or two, remember it will do us lots of good. We had a good letter from your daddy yesterday. With love and best wishes to you and your grandparents there and awaiting letters from both of you.

Sincerely,
Grandpa W.

These letters were more frequent during his illness and Mrs. Winger's illness and after her death during his loneliness. All reveal a tender concern for Vivian and the whole family. In his correspondence he makes frequent reference to the coming of Paul's or Robert's family and to other friends and relatives. And how he looked forward to their coming and enjoyed them when they came!

No doubt letters of a similar nature went to other members of the family. These are illustrative of his spirit. One of the memories he seemed to cherish was of Louann after Ida's death. He sent this story out in letters to various people.

North Manchester
2-23-1944

Louann's Prayer

Esther standing at the foot of the stairway heard Louann pray this prayer: she first speaks of her Grandma and is sorry she can't see her. Then she thanked Jesus for giving her a mother and a daddy who taught her about Jesus and the Bible and thanked him that her grandpa's and grandma's had taught her daddy and mother about them so that when she and Joe grew up they could teach their kiddies too. "Oh, Lord, I have forgotten sometimes, you know I do, but you know I love you and want to do the things you told us to do, so when I die I can come up and be with you and grandma in heaven, where you told us are many mansions you have made for us. Sometimes I think I'd like to come right away but mother says I must stay here first and learn to be good and help others to be good and love you. I miss my grandma and I love her but I know you will take good care of her. I would like to keep on talking to you all night but I must say goodnight. Goodnight Jesus. Goodnight God."

A very beautiful relationship existed between J. Oscar and President Otho Winger. It was a Jonathan-and-David kind of friendship. One needs to read the correspondence between them to feel the deep, intimate, affectionate regard they had for each other.

Otho was sixteen years older than Oscar. He was already president of Manchester College when Oscar entered. Oscar must have seemed like his son. After leaving Manchester, J. Oscar went to the Bluffton high school and the Muncie high school as a commercial teacher. He came to Manchester as a commercial teacher in 1922. He was a popular teacher in the commerce department. After ten years as a teacher he became field representative for the college. He was unusually well fitted for this position. As a genial, winsome personality with a glad smile, a warm handshake, and a slap on the shoulder he won friends for himself and the college everywhere. He visited high schools, churches, luncheon clubs, and young people's meetings and was welcomed. His visits to high schools were so much welcomed that people missed him when he ceased to come and asked for his return.

J. O. became a popular preacher. For many years he was a very popular evangelist going all over the college region and beyond it to hold meetings. For many weeks and many years he worked at the college during the day and drove out twenty, thirty, fifty, and even seventy miles nightly to hold meetings. He had a winning personality, a strong voice, deep earnestness, and an unusual faculty of quoting poetry.

Unfortunately his vigorous body began to break in the forties and after that he had to battle for his health and had occasionally to take time out for rest and recuperation; but he still did prodigious amounts of work and travel, driving at terrific speed.

Otho often wrote to friends that J. O. was doing two men's work. In June 1936, he wrote: "My brother, J. O. has gone to conference. He didn't want to go but he has done two mens work for the last two months, and I wanted him to go: so he is there at this time, and I hope he will stay until the meeting is over."

In many letters he frankly confesses that his own work would be impossible except for the great help from J. O.; certainly this must have been true, especially in the days after 1937 when Otho's health had begun to break. Oscar was feet and eyes and ears for him all over the college territory.

Save for the administration of the academic program, which was cared for by the faculty, J. O. could largely take over and do the work of the president.

Although Otho retired from college work in 1941, J. O. continued until 1943. Then for one year he was pastor of the church at Akron, Ohio, and one year at Nappanee, Indiana. Then he returned to live in North Manchester for short intervals between meetings and continued his evangelistic work until the time of his death on August 23, 1947.

Both Otho and Oscar made short trips to Florida to hold meetings and to build up their health in the Southern sunshine. During these separations frequent letters passed between them. While Oscar was pastor at Akron, Ohio, Otho wrote to him almost daily.

Interestingly, Otho was greatly concerned for Oscar's health and gave him the kind of advice he had very frequently received but scarcely ever heeded. On J. O.'s forty-sixth birthday Otho wrote:

I am concerned much for your safety and for your health. You are getting older too and in a dangerous age for men physically. . . . More important by far than getting a little more done is that you be careful against accidents and that you care for your health. This is my greatest concern. Neither the school nor the church nor myself can get along without your help.

At another time while J. O. was at Akron Otho wrote:

I know you will do much but you cannot do everything that is to be done. You will need to do much work in the library, preparing your messages. That will give your body some rest, but you will need some rest for your mind as well. . . . Don't work too hard in Akron; for a while start moderately.

And again he wrote: "We wish for you a safe trip to conference and a pleasant time while there. Be careful about any accidents. So many things might happen." These are sound warnings but scarcely what one would expect to hear from him.

In Otho's letters to J. O. there is the oft-repeated sentiment: "Be sure you have my thoughts and prayers every day for your work," or "You shall have our prayers and best wishes always." He encouraged J. O. also to spend time in his library. "Don't forget to take plenty of time for study," he wrote. And again: "I am glad you have some time to spend in your library; that will give you some rest physically."

It is not difficult to see why this warm, tender regard for each other existed. Otho had been like a father to J. O. To J. O., Otho was both an inspiration and an ideal. Here were two brothers in the ministry with deep interest in the church and in similar ideals. They had worked together for long years. The success of one was tied in with that of the other. When difficulties arose or when opposition appeared they confided in each other and gave each other moral support. Moreover, J. O. was to carry on in the ministry—following Otho, he hoped—and this gave him a keener interest in his work. The following quotations from letters reflect this relationship—almost too personal to record but they show best this very beautiful relationship.

In 1937 Otho wrote to J. O., "It has been such a busy year for you, made all the more so by the many things you have done for me. I appreciate it more than I can tell and hope some time to be able to repay it." In an undated letter, probably written about 1942, he said, "Yes, I am much interested in your work and think of you every day. I would have been most highly pleased if one of my boys had chosen the ministry. But since they have not, I am all the more interested in your work." And again in 1942 he wrote, "Since my days of work seem about over, at least active work, it gives me much pleasure . . . your receiving recognition and assuming responsibility."

Both men were unusually generous, not only in dealing with each other but in their relation to other men. They seemed to vie with each other to see which could be the more generous. When J. O. sent Otho a ten dollar check for additional pay for his services in a meeting he had held in Akron while J. O. was pastor there, Otho wrote to J. O. saying, "I enclose this ten dollars. I cannot receive it. The $100.00 I received was sufficient for my expenses and good pay for my work. Now I appreciate your liberal spirit, as you have always shown too much." And when Otho sent fruit from Florida for J. O. and others of the family, J. O., insisting on paying for it, said, "I know you like to be doing something for someone else all the time, and are not happy if you are not."

These sentiments in their own words are sufficient to indicate the affectionate attachment these two strong men had for each other. In their later days each was lost without the other.

The foregoing pages indicate the strong affection Otho had for his family. It is needless to say that all of them seemed to look to him as a great ideal.

Personal Qualities of President Winger

When Otho Winger was elected president of Manchester College there was very little organization at the college. There was no dean, no dean of men, no dean of women, no superintendent of buildings and grounds, and no personnel workers. There was a treasurer and a small faculty.

At the beginning of his administration President Winger spent his summers and many a week end in the field finding and recruiting students. When they came he often met them at the train and brought them to the college; he showed them to their rooms, often carrying their suitcases for them; he enrolled them in their classes, probably assigned them jobs, and taught not a few of their classes. Truly, it could be said of him that he was servant of all. No task was too difficult or too lowly for him. For a long time it was a practical joke about Manchester that the president carried the students' suitcases to the dormitory, and it was often a fact. He lived just across the street from his office—which was both fortunate and unfortunate. It was fortunate in that he could get to his work day or night quickly, but unfortunate in that he could never get away from it. At the close of his administration he said he felt he had been too close to the college.

From the time he took charge of the little struggling institution that Manchester was in 1911 until he resigned from the presidency of it in 1941 he never ceased to take a keen interest in the conduct and welfare of the individual student. He came to know the homes and the parents of many if not most of the students. In the earlier days of his presidency he helped to work out financial and housing arrangements for most of them before they arrived. He continued this for some to the end of his administration. In a letter in 1937 he wrote, "We have a full house, six-hundred-seventy or more. . . . I have had a personal conference with almost every student in school. It is a great opportunity, really a great joy to work with these young folks." Parents often wrote to him in advance, trustingly and confidingly hoping he would take a personal interest in their children. Many were grateful for a college like Manchester to which they could send their children and feel safe.

If students were sick he would visit them and write to the parents. If an accident or injury occurred he spared no pains or inconvenience to help. If students did poor work in college he attempted to learn the cause and then wrote to the parents. His letters are most interesting. Sometimes he would say, "The trouble seems to be that John just can't get grades. I don't know just why. Perhaps he just doesn't have the ability to do college work." Sometimes, "John just doesn't go to class. Unless he can make himself go to class and get his work he cannot expect to get better grades." Or, "The trouble is that Mary just doesn't settle down and study." In cases of this kind, he was exceedingly sympathetic with the parents and promised to help if he could.

For many, many years the president found his way almost daily into the dormitories. At the men's dormitory he might drop in almost any day or night—especially at night—and visit a boy's room. If noisy disturbances occurred in the dormitory he would be certain to appear, to the discomfiture of the culprits involved. Some boys could testify to the firmness of his grip when he came to the dormitory one dark night in the midst of a noisy outbreak and found the lights all turned off. One boy inadvertently ran into the president and afterward testified to the power of his grasp.

It is common knowledge to all who knew him that Otho Winger was an indefatigable worker. It is a tradition that will always be associated with his name. Only one endowed with an iron constitution, one blessed with boundless physical energy, could stand up as long as he did under the strain.

His letters and diaries reflect something of his long hours of work. To a friend he apologizes for not writing sooner and adds, "But constant daily work pressing one to the limit has prevented. Even now I am writing this near the midnight hour." Many of his letters begin with a reference to his long hours of work.

Necessity seems to have been laid on him and he seemed driven by an inner compulsion as if an unseen hand beckoned him on. His diary reflects many long hours. On June 8, 1914: "Busy in office, took boys to Grandpa Wingers. Talked late to Father. Wrote letters till 2 a.m." The next day: "Worked late as possible." On July 27, 1915: "Nothing but work." On May 11, 1923: "Returned home from Commencement thru the rain at 4 a.m." On January 1, 1924: "Another year. Happy New Year. I saw it come in and go out. Eighteen hours in the office. My work is such that when I leave, I rush extra until I go, then overtime after I return. Fifteen years of it already. How much longer?" On July 18, 1925: "Work in the office clearing up correspondence. Miss Harper leaves for vacation. Vacation—they say I should take one too. But—well there is so much needs to be done. Others can take their vacation. At least thirty calls and visits this week." On July 25, 1925: "Executive Board in the a.m., Galen Neher's funeral in the afternoon, write twenty-five letters at night." On March 7, 1930: "From Monday morning till this evening I have been on the go, I am very tired, I must rest a little."

He often went to the office before breakfast and worked awhile, returned after breakfast, worked all morning, all afternoon, and at night until twelve, one, or two o'clock. This schedule was followed for many, many years. William Meyers, who graduated from Manchester Academy in 1912, and was known as a hard worker, said he often worked until eleven o'clock at night and then being tired would stroll out over the campus for a rest and as he walked past "Prexy's" office and heard him pecking at his old typewriter he would return to his room and work for another hour or more.

It is not to be understood that President Winger

did mostly letter writing. He was all over the campus, and was likely to show up at unexpected places. He went down to the dining hall at mealtime, especially at the opening of the term. If tables had to be moved or chairs carried he did his share of the work. If there were special banquets involving many guests he was there to see that everyone was properly cared for. At homecoming, on May Day, or at commencement time he neglected nothing that would add to the comfort of guests. If students were sick he visited them. If someone had to be met at the train he often did it. If students had to be taken home he often did it himself. All this was in addition to the public work and responsibility he always carried.

At times there were critics who said that the president should employ a stenographer and save his energy, that he should leave more of the chores to others and save himself for the "big" things. He was aware of this criticism, and often defended himself by saying that there was no money to employ a stenographer. Whatever be the answer, the fact remains that he did not do it in his early years. He did most of his correspondence while others slept. It would have been difficult to secure a stenographer at those hours. And being made up as he was, it would probably have required greater effort to do this than to do the work himself. At least early in his administration he could not or would not delegate very much.

As he grew older and the school had become larger and had more money and still more work to be done, he employed a stenographer and gave up many of his duties to others. I think that he felt in his later years that he had given too many responsibilities over to others. Perhaps this was true.

President Winger was cast in a heroic mold—in every sense. Physically he was strong, rugged, massive, masculine. He had a strong voice. His voice carried well—too well at times. It could be heard through the halls and corridors, "booming," as some said. Once after the writer had become president of the college he heard loud talking in the hall during chapel. When he went to the hall to quiet the noise he found President Winger talking to one of the professors. There was no rebuke!

He had a massive head, heavy shoulders, square jaws, heavy eyebrows. His hands were small and rather delicate for so large a man. He had a keen sense of wholesome humor and enjoyed a joke, on himself especially. He had courage—physical and moral courage—and a heroic sporting spirit of adventure. He never dodged an issue or shrank from a duty because it was unpleasant. He seemed to enjoy an argument, but never for argument's sake. The surest way to get a quick "rise" out of him was to speak disparagingly of a friend, the college, missions, or any other cause which he championed.

But he was a square fighter. He never whimpered or engaged in self-pity. Charles D. Bonsack said to him in 1935, "It has always been a deep conviction of mine that you are one of the fairest and most honest men amidst your strong convictions that I have ever known and this makes it a pleasure to work with you even though we may sometimes have a difference of opinion."

President Winger was also rugged in his convictions of right and wrong. He had no sympathy with those who used sophistry to justify low standards of conduct and claimed that the old morality was outmoded. He insisted that there was no form of sin on which the ancients were uninformed; it was not a new form of morality which was being advocated now, but a low morality. "There aren't any new sins. Every sin that we have today existed at the time of Adam." There is a letter in his files, written to a man who had been greatly trusted and who had then fallen into gross sin, which sounds like the thunderings of a Hebrew prophet. He had no use for ministers of the gospel who were afraid to preach against sin. It was one of the disappointments of his later years that there was so much "pussy-footing" in the pulpit. Indeed, in every respect he was a rugged, forthright character.

His courage led him to deal directly, face to face, with anyone with whom he had a difference or a misunderstanding. His sense of fairness usually led to a satisfactory outcome. One of his teachers wrote to him:

Our close association in an administrative capacity has caused me to understand you better as well as to understand myself in a better way. The older I get, the more I realize how much value I have received from my experience in public life. One significant rule that I have learned is the rule of dealing directly with people with whom I am associated, both in terms of appreciation of their services and in terms of disagreeing with them if my judgment does not coincide with theirs. And as I have learned to know you more intimately, that is precisely the thing that you do—your directness of approach in the solution of problems is one that I hope to be able to match.

Sometimes his brusqueness in dealing with people of sensitive natures made him seem harsh and unkind. There were those whose spirits were wounded by his directness and seeming harshness. One of his critics went so far as to say, "He was not thoughtful of other people's feelings. He lacked gentleness and courtesy." And another said, "He was always hard on sensitive souls by his brutal frankness, but those who understood him, usually forgave and forgot." It is true that under great provocation he sometimes seemed terribly severe. But after the storm had passed he usually made up for it in extraordinary kindness and consideration. In a few cases he likely overreached in severity.

For instance, when three ministers' sons, all juniors, threw a hen bedecked with class colors into the chapel in the midst of a serious senior recognition day service, President Winger called all three of the boys to his office. The dean was also invited. Then he proceeded to tell those boys in language more forceful than elegant what he thought of their conduct. He reminded them of their fathers, who were elders in the church, and of what should be expected of boys who had such fathers.

The following summer one of the boys vowed he would not come back to the college as long as Otho Winger was president. But he did and later became one of President Winger's greatest admirers. In yet other cases of wrongdoing the severity of his punishment alienated young men, in a few cases permanently. This was, however, the exception rather than the rule.

One of his admirers said of him, "It has been my privilege to know no one who could forgive and forget, and who could receive back and be received back into full fellowship as easily and as readily as Otho Winger."

It could probably be said that those who knew him well enough and dealt with him often enough could overlook his harshness and know that there was an extremely just, and even tender and sympathetic, nature back of his seeming harshness and gruffness. This was certainly true during the period of the author's intimate association with him.

Otho Winger was distinctly an individualist. He was different. In early life, before he ever came to college, he was elected to the ministry in what some call the Dunker Church. It was then customary for Brethren ministers to go tie-less and wear the standing-collar clerical coat and a plain black hat with a wide rim. He donned that garb and came to college in it. And from this he never deviated. He went through college and university and served as president of the college wearing that distinctive garb. He attended all sorts of educational and other conventions, spoke at hundreds of commencements, and mingled with people of all kinds, but if he was ever self-conscious in regard to his attire his friends never knew it. In fact, he seemed so absorbed in living and working that his clothing received little thought. His wife sometimes chided him for not being more careful about his appearance, and I presume that some of his students and faculty wished he would give a bit more of his attention to the conventions of society. But his great spirit overcame these externalities and folks soon forgot them and appreciated him.

He was an individualist in other respects. At educational conventions, instead of joining with the crowd in a common hotel he often took a room in some near-by hotel and attended meetings when it suited him. The rest of the time he was either writing letters or some book or doing sightseeing on his own as at the National Educational Association convention in Boston in 1922.

He was not easily carried off by a fad. He thought for himself. He was unpredictable. One of the alumni wrote in 1928:

Some of us think we just about have it figured out what position you are going to take on specific issues and then you come along and do just the opposite. Last week is an illustrious example. There were all kinds of dire predictions around here about how you were going to block what some of us thought would make for progress.

I sat across the table awaiting the drop of the hat but when it had dropped several times it began to dawn on me that you were not looking for it. I think I have a new appreciation of your sense of honesty. I believe you have the right attitude and know that, if what was done will mean . . . progress, you had a significant part in it.

President Winger was an individualist in every way. His little lowly acts of unexpected kindness to students and faculty, his long hours in the office, his irregular habits of sleep, his fast driving—with an occasional automobile accident killing a cow or a horse and often nearly killing himself—his peculiar interest in old people, his Indian hobby, his thundering denunciation of sin and some sinners, and his tender ministrations to the sick or the bereaved soon developed a "folklore" about him. Among faculty and students and all over the college territory there developed a folklore about the unusual quality of the president of Manchester—most of it very kindly if not really affectionate—which was an asset both to him and to the college.

His personality was inimitable, his methods unique. And woe to a lesser man who tried to be like him or who, lacking like strength of personality, should attempt to use his methods.

DISCIPLINE

It is needless to say that the rules governing conduct at Manchester College were conservative from the first. At the turn of the century the church which Manchester represented was still strongly Puritanic. The members were to dress in plain attire; they were not to attend places of worldly amusement. The use of tobacco was frowned upon. Drinking of intoxicating liquor was entirely forbidden. Card playing was tabooed and dancing was not allowed. Women were not to adorn themselves after the foolish fashions of the world and were expected to wear a veil in religious services. The church as an official organization in this region took its stand for the most part on this conservative ground.

Otho Winger was a churchman. Furthermore,

he himself may be said to have been a conservative churchman. He took his stand with the church and attempted to conduct the college in keeping with the standards acceptable to the majority of the church.

In a letter to a friend in 1922 regarding another matter he defined his position on some of the distinctive practices of the church in these words:

From conviction, I was raised a Dunker. I have accepted her [the church's] principles and policies. I have promised to teach and practice them and accepted both my office and responsibility on that ground, and when I cannot continue I should state the matter plainly to the church and resign unless she wants me to continue. I believe that the Bible teaches these things . . . and I believe that there is need of a people who in simplicity follow the plain teachings of the church.

The issues changed from time to time but from beginning to end he was for maintaining the basic social ideals of the church.

He disliked card playing and believed cards were the gambler's tool. Early in his presidency he confiscated cards when he found them. In his later years he recognized that it was difficult to eliminate card playing entirely from the private rooms of students but it was forbidden in the social functions of the school. In 1932 he wrote to a co-worker, "I was taught that a deck of cards is a gambler's tool, I have found it so the world around. I believe it is wrong to play cards or to fool with a thing that has sent so many people on one of the worst paths of sin."

He was opposed to the use of tobacco among

college boys and girls. To a number of parents he wrote that he thought what got their boys into trouble was the use of tobacco. And in a case where a number of boys got into some other difficulty that led to disciplinary action, one of the conditions upon which they might continue in college was to cease smoking. He always discouraged smoking and during his administration forbade it on the campus, though students who smoked off campus were allowed to remain in college.

Drunkenness and theft came in for severe action. In the earlier days of his administration boys who drank or became intoxicated in college were required to make a public confession of their misdeeds. If they discontinued drinking they could remain in college. A continuance would result in their expulsion. Later the penalty might be different but no less severe.

Social dancing was forbidden on the campus. As a partial substitute for the dancing crave, President Winger instituted roller skating in the girls' gymnasium. He had the college purchase more than a hundred pairs of roller skates and these were rented to students at a nominal fee and skating became and remains popular. President Winger continued to preach and teach against these evils and Manchester drew many good students from other churches because it upheld these ideals.

He was also opposed to extremes in women's dress and made efforts to avoid them on the campus. He disliked bobbed hair because he believed that both Scripture and the rules of Annual Conference were opposed to it.

He insisted upon purity of life in matters of sex. Discipline was swift and severe upon those who gave evidence of being vicious in sex matters. In clear cases expulsion was the penalty. Often he, or the dean of women in the case of girls, accompanied young folks so disciplined to their homes to explain to parents. A letter of deep sympathy and regret always accompanied the announcement of expulsion.

In the last decade of his administration President Winger was very greatly disturbed about the laxity in matters of sex, and especially the teaching about sex in the country at large. In letters to some of his intimate friends he gave expression to his indignation because of the loose practice and the reckless teachings regarding sex. He wrote:

I heard a young man say in an open meeting, that he was not certain that promiscuous sex intercourse is wrong. He comes from a Dunker home, a member of a Dunker congregation and has spent some time in Manchester. When I asked him where he got this notion, he said it was all discussed at Lake Geneva in a conference conducted by Mrs. ———, a very fine worker with boys, prominent in camp work, etc. He said the boys discussed it pro and con in her presence. (The modern way and I think the devils way of opening the way to sin) that some boys from one or two of our colleges argued for it. I asked him whether she did not condemn such arguments. He said, "Oh, no. She merely said that she had a different ideal. . . ."

The thing that discourages one is that these things (various kinds of sin) are growing by leaps and bounds among our people and so few say anything about it. . . . I do confess that I hardly know what to say or think when I hear and know that we have so much worldliness in the church that is sapping the spiritual life out of us, out of our work, and that so little is said about it even by our preachers.

One of the strange contradictions in the life of President Winger was his severity in certain kinds of situations and his amazing patience and forbearance in others. Where there was gross sin, the violation of a sacred trust, persistent theft, or cases of persistent flaunting of the rules of morality and common decency, President Winger was exceedingly severe. Sometimes he seemed to forget for a little while how big and strong he was, and his wrath would flame forth in crushing fury. Those who heard these indignant outbursts were caused to tremble. But when they were over he could quickly forget and be restored to an easy fellowship with the party in question.

In other cases his patience and forbearance were so great that they led to the annoyance of the faculty. Many a boy was forgiven again and again. The president would secure a promise of improvement from him. If he erred again, he gave him another chance and yet others. In answer to critics he would say, "I know folks laugh at me, but if I can save one once in a while, I am willing to let them laugh at me." At President Winger's twenty-fifth anniversary, one alumnus said, "His investment of confidence in young men and women inspired and stimulated more honorable living in more different lives than will ever be known this side of eternity."

One of his best qualities in discipline was his ability to laugh at himself. If boys played a joke on him he would tell about it again and again and give a loud, hearty laugh. To this day one of the best-known pastimes of alumni of Manchester College is their gathering together in groups, telling one another about "the time Professor Winger caught a group of us" at this or that.

UNSELFISHNESS, MAGNANIMITY!

There was about President Winger an unselfishness, a spirit of generosity—even of magnanimity—that won for him the respect of all classes of people from the saints in the church to that group he sometimes called the "roughnecks." Though carrying the responsibility of the presidency, he often received less salary than some of his faculty. He was generous in dealing with his faculty when they had opportunity to earn extra money through lectures, extension courses, or otherwise. He was willing to carry the heaviest load, work the longest hours, and make the largest donations, and was happy about it. When a member of his family was in need he gave time, and, it is said, much money to help. A student or a parent in need found in him a friend. He often put himself to enormous inconvenience to drive people here or there. One Sunday morning, when his serious sickness of 1936 was beginning, he drove some Catholic students to early Mass at Huntington. In sickness or distress of any kind in the college or in the neighborhood he spared no sacrifice to be personally helpful.

In the spring of 1931, Mr. and Mrs. J. C. Brumbaugh of Hartville, Ohio, had visited the college, where their daughter was in attendance. On their way home, before reaching Fort Wayne, they had an auto accident killing Mrs. Brumbaugh and sending Mr. Brumbaugh to the hospital at Fort Wayne. On the day of the funeral at Hartville, President Winger went to Fort Wayne to spend an hour with Mr. Brumbaugh while his wife was being buried at home. Such thoughtfulness could not go unnoticed and unappreciated.

His complete devotion to the cause of his college resulted in his recognition of other people's worth to it. Any success or recognition that came to members of his staff made him genuinely glad. To one he wrote, "I shall be happy for whatever opportunity and recognition you may have in the future." These were not mere words. He gave abundant evidence that this was true. This is one of the severest tests of the real greatness of a leader. Little men cannot bear to see others rise around them who may threaten their leadership. This is the test which ultimately assigns second and third place to the near-great who fail at this point. In this test President Winger did not fail. He was generous in the recognition of the worth of others and magnanimous in his appreciation of them.

PUBLIC ACCEPTANCE

One of the questions difficult to answer regarding President Winger is "How do you explain his popularity? How can you explain his wide acceptance as a leader in so many situations?" He was elected president of Manchester College when thirty-three years of age. He was the youngest moderator of Conference ever elected up to his time, and he held that office six times. He was the first beardless moderator ever elected. How did he override that handicap? He was elected chairman of the General Mission Board when he was the youngest man on the board. In almost any group of men in the church or out, his leadership was recognized. But why? It is the opinion of the writer that it was a combination of qualities coming together in his personality that made of him a great leader.

He had a dominant personality. To repeat the words of Edward Frantz, he "looked and talked like a leader." Large of body, he had a strong voice, a massive head, strong shoulders, a genial face, vibrant energy, and an alert mind. He made a heavy impact on anyone who met him.

His mental processes were rapid. After having been a student under him, and then having worked on the faculty with him for more than a dozen years, I moved to another state and was gone for fourteen years. Upon returning and associating with President Winger again on occasion, I was tremendously impressed that even in his illness and crippled condition his mind still worked with lightning speed. His observations and responses were more rapid than those of any of his associates or co-workers, and his ability to put into a crisp and pithy saying some keen insight or wise observation was unusual.

It was his rapid-fire judgment and comprehension that gave him a great advantage in committee meetings, on the floor of Conference, or as moderator of Conference. His quick, intuitive insight, which was both keen and comprehensive and usually sound, was the marvel of such men as J. J. Yoder and C. D. Bonsack. It was this that helped outwit student pranksters. This quality won for him the admiration of his faculty and helped hold his leadership generally.

A third quality in him was his evident faith and sincerity. He believed in what he was doing. A letter to his most intimate friend reveals that he believed God was using him to do a great work at the college. He did not parade this faith but it was there undergirding his life. His faith in the church and her ideals was not feigned. It was genuine. The church was conservative, but so was he and by nature so. It was not mere diplomatic strategy in order to win support for the college that he insisted on staying close to the church. He would take his position squarely with the church and follow her ideals and practices. It was rather that the church represented his convictions. He believed, too, of course, that fair play, a sense of honesty, and common justice required that if a college drew support from a church it should correctly represent the church; or, in his words, "a college should take the cover off and let people see what we have at the college and these people will know to what and for what purpose they are giving." This was his attitude concerning both missions and the college.

President Winger also had a prodigious memory. This stood him in good stead. While teaching it was evident. He could give historical dates and require them *ad infinitum;* he could remember the names of all the kings and queens of Europe and all their cousins, uncles and aunts; he could name all the generals of the Civil War and the names of battles, and could give the names of rivers and creeks where battles were fought. He could recite poetry—long poems from end to end—to the wonder of his students.

This remarkable memory functioned to great advantage in his remembering the names of students, alumni, parents, and others. At Conference and local church meetings, to be able to call Robert or Jack or Mildred by name upon sight and recall some incident out of the past impressed them greatly and won their goodwill. Anywhere one goes in the college territory now one can hear "legends" of his feats of memory.

His unselfish interest in others won him an infinite number of friends. If parents learned of how he had visited their sick child, had helped him in trouble, or had driven him to the station or to Mass, they naturally came to appreciate him. He denied himself many a convenience and luxury in order to help others. Such evident unselfishness brings its rewards in public confidence and response. That such was his life we have shown elsewhere.

Furthermore his life was completely integrated and focused to one end. Whatever he did seemed to fit into a single pattern. *He had dedicated himself to the Kingdom of God.* Membership in it, said he, was the most important membership he had ever held. He valued it higher, he said, than any other honor that had ever come to him. He believed he could serve the Kingdom of God through Manchester College, through foreign missions, and through preaching. His whole life was integrated around that one ideal. To it he dedicated his whole life and energy, time, and talent.

Furthermore, he was not an introvert. He was never inclined to become introspective and spend time analyzing his inner moods and motives. He was an extrovert with a wholesome interest in and a keen enjoyment of the world of nature and the world of human affairs around him. He was an activist who was so busy doing things that he had no time to sit in morbid passivity and accuse himself because of what he was not.

There is yet one quality difficult to analyze or define which seems to the writer important. Probably it could best be said that Otho Winger had a remarkable ability to bring things to pass. When he became president, a college that seemed slowly dying came to life, students began to come, faculty members of strength appeared, buildings sprang up almost overnight, money began to come in, and public confidence increased.

Such buildings as the newer part of the administrative building appeared so quickly as almost to startle one. In 1926 the gymnasium-auditorium, the enlarged Oakwood Hall, and the improved heating plant were all dedicated in one great program at which Dr. M. G. Brumbaugh spoke.

An outstanding quality of President Winger was his ability to segregate a problem, give it his undivided attention for a time, and push it through to a conclusion, whether it was to publish a new bulletin, build a new building, handle a case of discipline, or any other problem. There are, of course, other factors that contributed to his success in bringing things to pass—such as his driving energy, his ability to win others to his support, and his ability to make them feel enthusiastic about his plans.

William H. Kilpatrick in 1921 in one of his classes once said that the fundamental plank in his philosophy of life was that "effort counts." In the last analysis it might be said that probably this, whether consciously so or not, was a fundamental plank in President Winger's philosophy also.

President Winger had great capacity for friendship. The qualities that made for this have already been partially described. In addition to those already delineated was that of being a good conversationalist. He loved people. He had a wide range of interests. He could engage in conversation about the great things of life, and could make "small talk" about the day-to-day happenings in a small community. I do not imply thereby that he was a gossip —he was not that. But he could find pleasure in that endless round of talk about home, school, church, children, marriage, sicknesses, crops, neighbors, and many other wholesome topics.

The range of his friendships was wide. He knew college and university presidents, the governor of the state, leading churchmen, school superintendents, and principals of high schools, but also a host of farmers, laboring people, merchants, sales people, and students. He was a friend of Tom Peabody, the millionaire manufacturer, of John Isenbarger, the small-town democratic politician, and of Ben Oppenheim, the leading merchant of North

Manchester, who said that Otho Winger was the best friend he ever had; and the appreciation of these men was mutual. The capacity to be "unselfconscious" in the presence of the great and the lowly was a rare gift which gave him great power with many people.

At Christmastime in 1925 the businessmen of North Manchester, in appreciation of what he had done for the college and thereby for the town of North Manchester, purchased and presented to him a Buick automobile. In response to this gift he wrote them a letter of appreciation, with praise for the splendid town and the promise of continued service in developing an institution that would be a credit to the town.

To our many friends, who well know our inability to own such a car of our own purchase, we have taken pleasure to explain that it was a Christmas gift from the businessmen of North Manchester. This, together with the information that you have been persistent and liberal givers to Manchester College has caused many elsewhere to appreciate your liberality.

President and Mrs. Winger maintained a special friendship with three other couples for many years. They were the Reverend Charles Smith and wife—Mr. Smith was for a time pastor of the First Methodist church of Fort Wayne; Homer Gettle, oculist and businessman of Fort Wayne, also a Methodist; and Dr. and Mrs. Charles Caylor of Bluffton, Indiana. One day a year they met and took dinner together and spent the day visiting. President Winger often spoke of his appreciation of these fine friends. To Dr. Gettle he wrote:

In fact, I appreciate very much these years of friendship, and the associations we have had. It is a great thing these days to be able to sit down and talk with a businessman and have him talk about spiritual things as you did this morning. I appreciate it very much; it was a great encouragement to me. I pray God's blessing upon your lay ministry such as you are doing.

The Kiwanis Club of North Manchester has at intervals granted to some citizen of North Manchester a Star of Service Award for outstanding service to the community. In 1941 the club presented this award to Otho Winger and placed his picture in the public library along with the other award winners—Tom Peabody, Jonas Warvel, L. D. Ikenberry, and J. R. Schutz.

In the presentation address it was said:

Everyone learning to know President Winger is impressed with his energy and activity. D. G. Mitchell once said, "There is no genius like the genius of energy and activity." Judged from this viewpoint Dr. Winger is a genius of highest rank. His life is proof that "a strong will, a settled purpose, and invincible determination can accomplish almost anything." Dr. Winger's close friend, William B. Bryan, once said one of the keenest pleasures that can come to any man is the pleasure that comes from knowing he has done a worth-while work and has done it well. Dr. Winger is receiving his reward in the knowledge that he has done his life's work well.

Otho Winger was indeed a great man, with a keen mind, a genial, winsome spirit, exhaustless energy, and a clear purpose. He had strong faith, deep convictions and great courage. He was unselfish, generous, and magnanimous. All his powers were focused to further the Kingdom of God.

Toward the Sunset

President Winger's health was rugged. It seemed for many years that his constitution must have been made of iron and that his energies were inexhaustible. Very few men could have stood up so long under the labor and strain to which he subjected his body. In his fifties, however, trouble began to appear.

For some time he had had some sinus infection which gave him distress. In his diary entry for February 28, 1930, he says, "Dr. Brubaker performs another operation on my head. Seemingly successful. This operation business for myself has become quite common." This indicates that there had been earlier ones. In late June it became serious. On July 1, he speaks of treatment by Dr. Kraning and Dr. Beaman—"much pain this evening." On July 6, he says, "Did not go to church because of sciatica." On the thirteenth he says he did not do much but go to the doctors and loaf after his office work was done. This sciatica evidently became so serious that he finally decided to go to Mt. Clemens, Michigan, for hot baths. He was there from July 20 to August 4. On the day he went, he says, he took eighteen anacin tablets. On July 27 he wrote, "Last Sunday so much pain it took twenty-four grains of anacin." Of the baths he says, "Water is so salty

your body floats, so mineral it is black. So hot it
. . . . Tromley [his attendant] says it doesn't hurt
him. I tell him he is hard boiled."

His pain left him and he went home on August
4. Within a week he was going full steam ahead
again, working at the office, traveling, preaching,
and lecturing.

Following this experience, President Winger
had more or less sinus trouble occasionally, although
in his *Memories of Manchester* he wrote: "I have
always been blessed with good health. I scarcely
knew what it was to be sick until I was fifty-eight
years old. Whatever weaknesses I have had have
come from my own mistakes and over work." During the next half dozen years he continued an amazing program of work—office work, mission board
work, sermons, funerals, and commencements, along
with trips to educational conferences and Annual
Conference.

On Saturday, April 4, 1936, his diary records
that he worked "all day in the office until midnight.
Have headache in the evening." The next day he
drove a college girl to Mass at Huntington early
in the morning and preached at the Baptist church
in Marion in the afternoon. "Terrible headache, call
Dr. Beaman," says the diary that day. On Monday,
April 6, he went to Chicago on the morning train to
sit for a portrait being painted by Paul Trebelcock.
"I am sick. Terrible night at New Weston Hotel,"
says his diary. The next day he was too sick to sit
longer for Trebelcock; so he returned and went to
the Bluffton Clinic and remained all night at the
Wells County Hospital. He remained here for two

days more, then went home but was no better. He canceled his engagement to preach at the Yellow Creek church on the Sunday following, and returned to the clinic every day. On April 14, the doctors gave their reluctant consent for him to go to an Elgin board meeting. He went on the fifteenth, attended board meetings two half days, and returned on the sixteenth. On the seventeenth he went to the clinic and arranged for an operation the next day, but gave a commencement address at Argos that evening.

The doctors had earlier discovered a closed ethnoid sinus. This they had opened but a pocket of pus had formed in his head. They operated to remove the pocket of pus on April 18, and then there followed a period of terrible sickness, hemorrhages, and extreme weakness, requiring blood transfusions. For two weeks he was very ill, and the doctors almost despaired of his life. He remained at the hospital for five weeks and even after his return he fainted from weakness upon exertion. He managed to muster enough strength to return to his home to participate by his presence in the celebration of his twenty-fifth anniversary as president of the college.

Soon he was back at work again, but he continued to have difficulty with his eye. His letters frequently made mention that his health was better but that the sight of his eye was not returning. It continued to give him constant trouble and finally threatened the sight of his other eye; so in the spring of 1938 he had the eye removed. Within a very few days after its removal, he had his oculist friend,

Dr. Gettle, provide him a glass eye, and the next day he was off by auto to Lawrence, Kansas, to Annual Conference. But his health did not fully return. He continued a heavy program of work. In the spring of 1940, on May 1, he made a trip to Earlham College, where he gave an address, then went on to Dayton and Gettysburg, Ohio, and back. On the next day he wrote, "Sciatica bothering me more." The next day, "Left side numb. J. O. took me to the Caylor Nickel Clinic and hospital where I remained for a week. They call it peripheral paralysis." The paralysis affected his left hand, his left leg, and his speech. One can see the effects of the paralysis in his handwriting in the diary from the very day it seriously affected him. From this he never fully recovered. Though he was able to get about and do some of his work, yet from here on he was seriously handicapped.

In the spring of 1940, he announced to the board of trustees his purpose to retire a year later. He and his wife had moved to the west end of town in 1939. To this home, called Maple Oaks, they now retired, and here they spent their last days.

In the summer of 1943, President Winger seemed to suffer a slight stroke of apoplexy. This, added to his earlier afflictions, had a devastating effect on his health and on his personality. While he continued semi-active for a time, those who were near him could observe that only occasionally would the Otho Winger of former days shine through.

In the meantime, Mrs. Winger's health had been declining. Her hip affliction, which had required an operation about once in five or six months, now required surgery about once in five or six weeks, and each of these experiences was not only extremely painful but weakening. In the summer of 1943 she grew worse. It now appeared that she was also suffering from diabetes; then followed a week of influenza about Christmastime, and after that an attack of inflammation of the liver (hepatitis). She was taken to the hospital at Bluffton for a time, returned to her home for a week at her request, and was then taken back to the hospital, where she quietly passed away on January 29, 1944. She was buried in the Pleasant Hill cemetery by the West Manchester Church of the Brethren, near the home of her childhood.

Soon after her death Otho wrote the previously mentioned fifty-page booklet, *In Memory of Ida Miller Winger,* which tells the story of her parentage, her school days, their life and travels together, their home, family and friends, and her sickness, death, and burial. It breathes a tender spirit of appreciation of her who had borne the heat and burden of the day's work with him.

The death of Mrs. Winger was a severe shock to him. One of the poets has said that quiet to active souls is hell. Suffering in body, almost helpless because of paralysis, doomed to inactivity, this great man was now faced with the added burden of loneliness. Bereft of the one he had loved most deeply, he was terribly lonely.

He and Edith, Mrs. Winger's younger sister who had lived with them many years, now lived together in the old home which Mrs. Winger had inherited from her parents. Mrs. Winger had said

to him on her deathbed, "Take good care of Edith."
He gave her a home, but she took care of him more
than he could care for her.

At times he was quite active and alert and was
his usual self. At other times he seemed morose and
dejected, and his mind seemed far away.

At last his body deteriorated and broke under
the ravages of disease. He grew much worse early
in August and was taken to the Wabash County
Hospital. It seemed that the great giantlike strength
of his body found it hard to let go of the spirit. That
which was earthy clung to that which was eternal.
A mighty struggle ensued, but the end came in the
evening of August 13, 1946.

His body was taken to the home where many,
many friends came to look on the form of him who
so often had comforted others in their bereavement.
Funeral services were conducted by the author at
the Walnut Street Church of the Brethren, assisted
by Dr. R. H. Miller of the college and Dr. C. C. Ellis
of Juniata College. The text of the funeral sermon
was taken from the words of St. Paul, which seemed
to suggest themselves by the nature of his life: "I
have fought a good fight, I have kept the faith. I
have finished the course—henceforth there is laid
up for me a crown of righteousness. . . ."

He was buried by the side of his beloved Ida.
The tombstone with its legend had already been
arranged by him. Here, among many whom he had
helped lay away, peacefully rests the form of him
who had taken so little time on earth to rest. Here
come many to view the last resting place of one
they loved and admired.

A Crowned Life

PRESIDENT OTHO WINGER'S FUNERAL SERMON
By V. F. Schwalm

Scripture lesson: 1 Peter 1: 3-9. Texts: 2 Timothy 4: 7-8; 2 Corinthians 5: 1; Job 19: 25-27.

We are met this afternoon to honor the memory of an extraordinary man. He was a man who arose from the ranks of common men, whom he loved and understood as few men have. He never lost the common touch. Yet he so lived and worked in his day that he stood in power and influence among the great men of his generation. To many of us he was an intimate friend and counselor and, in a sense, a godfather. Thousands of other hearts, those of churchmen and students, are turned this way at this hour in grateful memory for his past friendship and kindnesses.

For the past few years our brother has had to wage a long, lonely, and stubborn battle against the ravages of disease. These have been difficult and discouraging years, sentencing him to suffering and to inactivity most unnatural to him. Though he faced his suffering bravely and bore his inactivity courageously, those who knew him only during these days did not know the greatness of the man in activity. Life must be seen in perspective. There

273

were more than sixty years of relatively good health, vigor and intense activity. These should not be forgotten. The tone, the tenor, and the quality of his life must be taken during his fighting years—the years of health, of labor, and of achievement.

"I have fought the good fight." When St. Paul came to the end of his life, he had the satisfaction of having fought a good fight. Paul had achieved mightily for his Lord in the face of overwhelming opposition. He worked faithfully; he had a sense of the urgency in life. "Woe is me if I preach not," he said. "I am all things to all men in order that I might by all means save some." He suffered affliction of the body, he endured opposition, he was mercilessly persecuted, and he was left for dead, but he carried on in spite of all these. At the end he had the satisfaction of knowing that he had fought a good fight.

There is great satisfaction in the consciousness of having fought life's battles well. Naturally one wants to win in the battles of life. But win or lose, the consciousness of having fought well, of having fought faithfully and fairly, is a source of great inner happiness. The man who wins without this knowledge does not enjoy the sweetness of victory. The man who loses with the knowledge that he has fought well has consolations in his loss. To win and know that one has fought a good fight is a source of double joy.

President Winger was a good fighter in the battle of life—in the sense that Paul meant it. He seemed to love challenging jobs and he attacked them with all the vigor of his rugged personality. I never knew a man who seemed to get so much pleasure out of his work, out of the mere expenditure of energy, as he did. In a letter written to me on October 23, 1927, he said, "One's greatest joy and credit comes only as he gets it out of the work with which he is identified. So if that work prospers, that is sufficient for reward." This sounds like St. Paul, who said, "Let every man prove his own work, and then shall he have rejoicing in himself and not in another."

President Winger was not only a good fighter but he admired others who met life squarely and bravely and also fought nobly and courageously. He loved an opponent in argument who put up a strong opposition. Many of us can testify that he inspired us to attack jobs which we would not have had the faith to tackle if it had not been for his encouragement.

He carried on his heart the burden of great causes—his family, his church, the college, and foreign missions. His devotion to his family is too well known and perhaps too personal for comment here.

He had a sincere, lifelong interest in the church. Among my first memories of him are those of seeing him driving out from the college on Sunday to some rural church to preach there. The welfare of the churches was his constant concern. The evident genuineness of his interest in the church resulted in great confidence in his leadership. Increasing responsibilities were entrusted to him. He traveled far and near to preach funerals, to dedicate churches, and to speak at Conference and on other special

occasions. On the Conference floor as a parliamen-
tarian he had no equal in his day. Six times he was
called to be Conference moderator. For thirty years
he was on the General Mission Board, during sixteen of which years he was its chairman. He gave
of his thought and his effort to promote the welfare
of the church. It can well be said of him as Paul
once said, "There is that which presseth upon me
daily, anxiety for all the churches." Surely for the
church he fought a good fight.

He was elected to the presidency of Manchester
College in 1911. The college was small, struggling,
its future uncertain. He saw the college as an agent
of the church, a means through which to serve God
and the Kingdom. To this cause he now dedicated
every ounce of his boundless energy and served
that cause with a devotion and selflessness scarcely
equaled in my experience. The student body grew
by leaps and bounds, buildings were erected, the
faculty strengthened. This job alone would have
been a credit to any man.

President Winger seemed to sense that the college could grow and prosper only as it served young
people. So he set a worthy example of humble service to young people in so many ways that it has
become a tradition. His interest in and service to
the humblest student is known everywhere. As
one travels among the alumni, he can hear new
stories of his helpfulness every day. His name is
blessed by the lips of thousands of students for
kindnesses done. At President Winger's twenty-
fifth anniversary one alumnus said, "His investment of confidence in young men and women has

inspired and stimulated more honorable living in more different lives than will ever be known this side of eternity."

But his influence did not stop with his own church and school. It reached throughout the community and the state. His name was respected and revered by the strong men of the state in other colleges, in the universities, in political circles, and in civic life. Surely, this good man had a right to look back over his achievements in church, in school and community and say, "I have fought the good fight," though he would have been too modest to say it.

"*I have finished my course.*" Very few men, if any, come to the end of life with a sense of having finished their work. We come to the end of a year with some things undone that we had hoped to do. We come to the end of life like the shepherd in Wordsworth's poem—with "an unfinished sheepfold." I think that if President Winger could speak, he would say, "There were still some things I had hoped to get done."

But in another sense life is like a relay race. In fact, the most recent translation of this phrase is "I have finished the race." One man takes the torch and carries it to the next, and then drops out of the race, while another carries it on, and then he too drops out. All together they run the race. Each man has his share of the journey to run. If he runs his race well and furthers the cause, he has done his part.

Doctor Winger came to North Manchester, to Manchester College, and into responsibility in the church when he was a relatively young man. He was trusted with great responsibility. In the thirty-five or more years since then he has set forward the work of the church immeasurably. He has given life, vigor, and hope to a college that might otherwise have disappeared. The work of the church is not completed; the college is not made perfect. Other causes he served are incomplete. But he has finished his part of the program; he has carried the burden for his part of the race. It is now for other hands to take up where he has left off and carry on.

In the president's poetry classes some thirty years ago we learned that "we are the heir of all the ages, in the foremost files of time." We stand on the shoulders of the race. It is our task to build on what our fathers have left us. I recall him quoting Browning as saying,

> Progress is man's distinctive mark alone,
>   Not God's, not the beast's,
> God is, they are,
>   Man partly is but wholly hopes to be,

or Tennyson,

> Yet I doubt not through the ages one increasing purpose runs,
> And the minds of men are widened, through the process of the suns.

Could he speak now, he would probably say, "My work is finished. The work must go on. Other hands must carry the load now." However reluctant we may be to attempt the heavy loads he carried, it is our task to do our bit to carry the torch, to further the causes for which "he gave the last full measure of devotion." He himself has gone to join the immortals of our church, of the community.

"*I have kept the faith.*" The faith Paul kept was the Christian faith. He accepted it on the Damascus road. Then all the pride of race and class, of training and self-righteousness, he counted but loss for his faith in Christ. And that faith kept him, and he kept it—to the end.

From then on the Christian faith became the whole of his life. It absorbed every other interest. It motivated him to tireless efforts for the Kingdom of God. It drove him over land and sea to proclaim the good news of the gospel. It became the center and focus of all of his life, integrating his powerful personality around this one supreme purpose. He kept his faith through persecution of every kind, for he could say, "I know in whom I have believed, and am persuaded that he is able to keep that which I have committed unto him against that day." He was assured that when the earthly house of this tabernacle was destroyed he had a building not made with hands, eternal in the heavens.

President Winger too was a man of deep religious faith. He became a Christian early in life. He seems always to have been busy in the work of the church. Religion was not feigned or assumed on special occasions. It was part of the warp and woof of his daily life.

President Winger's faith was a practical faith. His was not a cloistered faith. He was not primarily a mystic who withdrew from society in contemplation and devotion. His was not a weak, sickly faith, pale and anemic. It was a strong, rugged faith of action, a faith that manifested itself in carrying heavy loads, doing acts of kindness, visiting the sick, helping the poor, carrying suitcases, comforting homesick students.

As one who has known President Winger for nearly forty years, I have never had occasion to doubt the genuineness and reality of his faith. I recall how often he chose for the chapel hymn *Precious Name, O How Sweet,* or *My Faith Looks Up to Thee,* or some other deeply spiritual hymn of the church, on which his strong voice rang out.

It was a positive faith. It seemed at times a simple faith though not an unintelligent faith. Those who took his philosophy course knew that he knew all the doubts and questions of the philosophers, but he kept his faith, a faith that brushed aside finespun speculative arguments of little relevance and clung to the truths by which men live.

President Winger kept a rugged faith in the importance of the good life. He did not allow himself to be misled by the sophistications that explain away ethical distinctions. He kept the lines between right and wrong, between good and evil, clear. And he was uncompromising in his attitudes. At Nampa, Idaho, in 1937 I heard him say, "The older I get, the less I care for brilliant men, or clever men, and the more I admire good men." This impressed me greatly as representing his attitude in all of his life. President Winger's powerful influence for righteousness will live on as long as his memory continues.

In all these respects President Winger kept

the faith. At Colorado Springs in 1931, he said, "I have membership in many organizations. But I belong to no organization whose membership I prize as much as my membership in the Kingdom of God." As I knew him, that represented the true testimony of his life. I can still hear him sing, "I love thy church, O God. . . ."

What was the nature of the faith that he kept?

He kept faith in the love, the goodness, and the overruling providence of God. Many can remember these lines on his lips:

> Yet in the maddening maze of things
> And tossed by storm and flood,
> To one fixed trust my spirit clings,
> I know that God is good.

He believed in the deity and the atoning death of Christ. I can still hear his voice as he read for us Tennyson's ringing words:

> Strong Son of God, Immortal Love,
> Whom we who have not seen Thy face
> By faith and faith alone embrace,
> Believing where we cannot prove.

He believed in the Bible, knew it thoroughly, and used it effectively. He might well have written this line: "Blessed Bible, how I love it."

He believed in future rewards and punishments, "that every man must give an account of himself to God."

He believed in immortality, and in many a funeral quoted those well-known lines of Whittier:

> Alas, for him who never sees
> The stars shine through his cypress trees,
> Who hopeless lays his dead away,

Nor looks to see the breaking day
Across the mournful marbles play,
Who hath not learned in hours of faith
The truth to flesh and sense unknown,
That life is ever Lord of death
And love can never lose its own.

He kept the faith. Though, as with Job, it may have been difficult through his suffering to see God's guiding hand, *he kept the faith.*

"I have fought a good fight, I have finished my course, I have kept the faith. Henceforth there is laid up for me a crown of righteousness. . . ." This figure of speech is taken from the Greek custom of rewarding a runner in their races with a crown. Paul says he anticipated a crown of righteousness. Just all that that meant to him I do not know. But certainly you and I would agree to crown Paul and remember him as a righteous man. So our brother will live on in our memories as a great, good man. In the gallery of great men in our room of memory we will give him a place, and say—and continue to say—wherever we speak of him, "Here was a good man."

As I travel and mingle with men—all kinds of men, farmers, laboring men, old men, old women, alumni, other college men, university men, businessmen—over the same territory in which he traveled they crown him with the words, "He was a good man—a great man."

And we have faith that his Lord, too, has said to him, "Thou hast been faithful; come up higher."

May I personally testify that apart from my own father no man had as much influence over my life in those days when my life was in the making, when I made my choices.

Most of us do not have the ability to do all that President Winger did. But we can emulate his virtues:

1. His love for all kinds of people;

2. His humble service to our fellow men;

3. His uncompromising loyalty to the right;

4. His devotion to his Lord.

May the memory of his life be a benediction to his children and grandchildren, and to them and to us all we would commend that we, too, keep the faith which sustained him in his endeavors.

Notes from President Winger's Diary

I am here including notes from President Winger's diary just as he wrote them. They are not evenly distributed through the years but are somewhat typical of his entries. As indicated in the text of the book, he very often refers to the chapel speakers, to the number enrolled in the college, to preachers at the church, to the outcomes of games, to public affairs such as the wars and the deaths of public characters, to funerals he preached, to commencement addresses he gave with the subjects he used, and to matters pertaining to his family.

1914

July 24. Anniversary of our wedding, July 24, 1902. Funeral services of Elder Daniel Snell. Aged nearly 76 years. Elder John Wright preached the funeral. Pall bearers: G. L. Studebaker, Henry Neff, Em. Leckrone, J. C. Murray, A. C. Young, and Otho Winger. Large crowd. Elder Snell ordained Otho Winger to Eldership Nov. 11 . . . . In the evening, D. B. Garber and Manly Deeter came. Conference over building. Elder and Mrs. Garber remained over night. Official meeting at Church. Ohio program in Chapel.

July 27. I went swimming with boys in evening.

July —. News of European war grows daily more discouraging. Austria attacks Servia, because of Servian influence in assassination of Prince Ferdinand. Russia is inclined to attack Austria. The Triple Alliance and Triple Entente may involve all Europe.

August 3. War clouds thicken in Europe. We pray that peace may abound.

August 5. Germany and England war against each other. Germany at war with most of Europe. Sentiment in history class much against Germany.

August 12. Mamma is not feeling well; Paul is hoarse. Robert cut big gash in his head. Papa is worn out.

August 20. All day Board Meeting at Elgin. Returned home the same evening leaving Elgin at 10:00 p.m. and Chicago at midnight.

August 22. Busy in office till evening. I went to Father Winger's in eve. Mamma and boys remained at home. Mother Winger not at all well.

September 5. Mended chicken house. Built rabbit pen. Several persons called. Mother Winger came at 11:00.

September 11. School is going well.

September 26. We take dinner at home this Sunday. We wonder what is to be the outcome of the great battle of Aisne, now in progress.

October 8 (at district meeting). Elected reading clerk and on S. C. [Standing Committee].

November 9. Dr. Conwell of Phil. in Chapel. "Acres of Diamonds."

December 2. D. R. McFadden preaches a great sermon. "What do ye more than others?"

December 13. Meeting's still in progress, six came today. 38 in all. Snowy and stormy.

December 28. Spent the day in the Dayton Public Library.

1915

January 3. At Church on Walnut Street. J. C. Murray preached a great sermon. At dinner at Mother Winger's.

January 13 (Wednesday). A rousing Educational

Meeting held. The Living Endowment plan started. $6500 subscribed. E. B. Bagwell, G. S. Strausbaugh, J. F. Brubaker, Manly Deeter spoke. Bagwell's speech was unique.

January 30 (Saturday). Forenoon in office. Went to Mexico in evening. All night with Frank Fishers.

January 31 (Sunday). A rainy day. Preached twice, Texts: Acts 1:8, Samson. Ate dinner at Irvin Fishers.

February 1. Canvassed Mexico Church. At dinner at Will Rush's. All night with John Miller's.

February 2. Canvassed. Very good success. Came home in evening. Found all well.

February 4. This has been a great day at the College. Everything seems to go just right.

February 10. Little sleep but much worry!

February 12. A new case of small pox.

March 14. J. H. Wright preached a good sermon. A. L. Wright preached a good funeral sermon for Mrs. Isaac Cripe.

March 15. Visited schools at Laketon and Roann. In evening went to Milford. Visited Manly Deeter.

March 16. Visited Milford schools [and] Goshen College. Went to Bryan, Ohio, in evening. Stayed all night.

1916

January 1 (Saturday). This is a dark cheerless looking day, but the sun will shine.

—Another incident—

Paul had had some trouble in school. He did not want to go back in the afternoon, but was told he must. As he burst forth in a sigh he said, "*I wish I were a dog.*"

February 19. Nothing unusual until evening. When Lincoln's and Majesticos prevented Adelphians from having a program in the Chapel. There seems to be considerable of the savage left in us. . . .

February 22. A little explanation in the Chapel was necessary to get students to see the reason for some Executive Board Regulations.

October 15. At home for the first time in twelve weeks on Sunday.

1917

February 12. Rain. Went to Wabash and Somerset. Funeral of Mrs. John Strausburg Job 1:27— Wreck on way home. Rode horseback to Wabash.

February 13. Busy at home. Sore over trip.

February 15. Loves sweet dreams. Mamma helps prepare for convention. Scarlet fever—quarantine.

March 23. In office, worked around barn in P.M. World's greatest battle on in France.

March 28. The chief war news of the day is that the Allies are holding. Hurry up call to America.

April 12. May the God of battles and of Peace soon end this struggle rightly.

June 9. Helped organize Standing Committee. Studied.

July 17. Another great German drive report. Quentin Roosevelt killed. Anxious for tomorrow. Hard at work in office.

August 2. Reports of great French American victory.

November 7. False news about Peace. Nation goes wild.

1918

November 11. 1:45 a.m. Germany signs Peace Armistice. Now 3:30. Everything is blowing. A big demonstration downtown.

1920

February 8-9. Smallpox suspected.

February 11-27. Quarantined for smallpox.

June 7. H. C. Early came. Sadie's wedding. H. C. Early preached.

June 8. H. C. Early at Chapel. At our place for dinner and supper.

September 8. Run nail in foot.

September 9. Very great pain. Dr. Cripe here.

September 10. In bed all day for first in memory.

1923

March 25. Preached at Walnut Street both morning and evening on the History and Message of the Church of the Brethren. Visited Amos B. Miller, Levi Miller, John Hoover, Luther Brubaker, George Lukenbaugh.

April 8 (Sunday). Preached at Walnut St. on "Forbidden Fruit." Official Council in afternoon. Jos. Neher died in the morning. Calls at John Cupp, Walter Warner, Sherman Bakers.

April 9 (Monday). Work on Church lists. Robert and Lucille brought baby, Vivian home from Ohio. She is not so well.

April 10 (Tuesday). Paul is 16 years old today. Is it possible he is that old. Jos. Neher buried. Official Council at the Church. Ashland College Girls Glee Club.

April 12. We have committee meetings to consider enlarged athletics. The papers are filled with news of the closing of Goshen College.

April 29. At Greenville. Morning Missionary sermon. Evening to Young People. Home 105 miles without a stop.

August 22. With Mamma, Hazel and Etta Brooks and Virgil Finnell went to Salamonie. Returned at night. Auto accident near Ogans Creek Church. What might have been????? Mother's arm broken. We reached home at 1 p.m.

September 22. Institute at Bourbon and Plymouth. Robert with me. We drove from Plymouth to Hart, Michigan, arriving at J. J. Scrogums at 1 a.m.

September 25. L. D. Ikenberry led Chapel. Call to preach.

October 23. Forty-six today. It seems so short a time since I recorded the forty-fifth birthday. Older people say that 45 is still young. I shall feel that it is. I do feel that it is, but 20 years more will place me among the older. And it seems so very short a time since 20 years ago.

November 28. School closes for the fall term. It has been a great term of school. 515 enrolled. Excellent results.

December 1. On way down [to Flora], my Mother and I stopped at Geo. Swiharts to see the remains of Ray Mishler, killed at Camden, Wed. Morning. So young and so useful.

December 31. The Old Year is going. Like all other years. Many matters of interest. Not so victorious. Future not so bright but we face it doing duty as best we can. Farewell 1923.

1924

January 1. Another year. Happy New Year. I saw it come in and go out. Eighteen hours work in office. Students return for school.

February 1. Attend Ft. Wayne - Manchester basketball game. Manchester wins. Paul is pleased. Report that Woodrow Wilson is dead.

April 30. The mid-spring term enrollment complete. The largest enrollment in the history of Manchester. 621 students. A very fine class of folks. Seniors took a day off.

June 2. To Philadelphia via Reading. Visited places of interest. University of Pennsylvania, Independence Hall, Carpenter's Hall, Betsy Ross House, Franklins Grove, Germantown, and Church of the Brethren. Talked with Miss Swigart and Cedric Eichelburger. All night at Hotel Reading.

September 20. Worked in office in forenoon. In the potato patch in p.m. Middle Indiana Young Peoples Conference on.

December 31. Gone—gone in a hurry. We would not recall it though it means one year less of life. Not how many years shall we live but how shall we spend them.

1925

January 1. Students had returned and spent the last day of the year in study. A pleasant evening together in open Dormitory by the girls. The New Year found several hundreds of us in the Chapel to see the New Year in. A few hours sleep and the first day of the Year. We had an excellent Chapel talk. A heavy snow fell in the afternoon.

August 9. Preached at Walnut Street. Made calls at 25 places during the day. Loren Ohmart died in the evening.

October 23 (Friday). I am 48 today. Lawrence will be 35 tomorrow. We have dinner together. Mother, Oscar's. Lawrences here. Students come and sing in evening.

October 25 (Sunday). Mrs. Frances Arnold died this morning. Lizzie Brooks is very bad sick. We visited at both places. Went to Marion at 1 p.m. We visit the Indian family, The Winters. Had not seen some of them for nearly 30 years. Robert, Tilly, Lilly, William. We went on to Southern Ohio to see Lucille and Vivian. A good visit.

October 26 (Monday). Drove to Earlham College, Richmond. Thru to Oxford, Ohio. Visited in different college homes of Miami university. Saw Oxford College and Western College. Then thru Brookville, Ind. to Hope. We had not been here for 9 years. Saw many old friends.

October 27 (Tuesday). Drove home. Helped preach funeral of Mrs. Arnold. Many things to look after.

October 28 (Wednesday). Mamma and I s t a r t again at 5 a.m. We were to Indianapolis by 8:30. Visited Indiana Central at University Heights. Visited Franklin College at Franklin. On through Columbus, through Brown County. Visited Bloomington and various places there. Left Bloomington at 3:30 p.m. South through Lawrence County. Beautiful scenery. Bedford, Mitchell, Paoli, West Baden. A wonderful hotel at West Baden. French Lick, Jasper, Oakland City by 9 p.m. Found M. McMillen sick. 300 miles today.

October 29. Visited Oakland City College. A unique institution. Visited Evansville College. Took dinner at Cafeteria with Prof. Humke. Drove on to Mt. Vernon on beautiful Ohio. New Harmony where Rapp and Owen lived. On to Vincennes. Dark and snowing. Saw some things of interest. Left at 6 p.m. thru Spencer to Greencastle. 250 miles today.

October 30. Drove around DePauw's Buildings. Great. Drove to Danville, Central Normal. A good gymnasium. On home until 12M. Too much snow for College outing. College entertainment in evening.

October 31. Many things to be done today. Football game. Muncie 14, M. C. 7. Homecoming. In the evening I went to Lima by train. Rest of night at hotel.

November 1. Dedication of Pleasant View. Gen. 35: 2. A very large crowd here. In evening "The Second Mile." In Lima, I stayed with Dave Weaver till 1:30 a.m. Home via Penna. and Warsaw.

1926

December 31. And now at midnight I sit writing the last record of the year. The last year has gone so rapidly. How will the coming year be? We welcome you, 1927.

1928   (Notes made in India)

March 12. Monday, District Meeting. G. V. Satvedi. Dr. R. B. Jerome. A good moderator. A good meeting. Held in a tent. People sat on the ground. 19 native delegates. Some talkative. The moderator wore dhoties. Meeting closes at 5: 00 p.m.

March 19. The Missionary Conference closes, Anklesvar. Missionaries have many problems and many differences just the same as other people at home. With all their problems they are doing a remarkably fine job of work.

March 24. A great crowd welcomes us [to Vyara] with garlands. We rest at girls' compound. Then to love feast in evening. 400 members commune.

March 25 (Sunday). 200 others there to be fed. In the morning I preach to a large crowd. Many natives have walked here 5 to 20 miles.

April 9. This is our last day in Anklesvar. We are getting ready to leave. 31 years ago today I was elected to the Ministry. Time flies. We eat dinner with the girls. Washing and packing.

April 11. Bombay is a great city. But it is hot. Very warm.

1929

June 1 (Saturday). Another school year ended. It has been a great year for hard work. Much accomplished. Some rest.

June 22. One year ago today we landed in San Francisco [from] a world trip. The year has been short but filled with hard work. The trip has receded far into the background. We are glad for the chance to work at home. Now with a few days rest and as the days grow longer more work must be done.

July 24. This is our 27th wedding anniversary. Take dinner at Dining Hall with J. Edson Ulreys, A. B. Ulrey, etc. The years have flown. We recall July 24, 1902. Many were living then who are not now. Many souls are now in existence who were not then. Time is winging us away to our eternal home.

August 5-9. This has been one of the most successful terms in the history of Manchester.

September 7. I. B. Book sickens and dies. Sick from 7 A.M. to 2 P.M. A great surprise and shock.

October 13. Wrote letters to Ramsey MacDonald and Herbert Hoover commending their program of peace and good will. Ramsey MacDonald commended for coming to America on Mission of Peace.

November 28. After working late last evening we start for Detroit at 2 A.M. Find Doctor and family in wreck near the Comstocks. Bring them to town and then on and on. Detroit by 9 A.M. Thanksgiving dinner at Roberts.

1930

March 7. From Monday morning till this evening I have been on the go. I am very tired. I must rest a little.

July 7. Forty years ago today Father Winger was hurt. Forty years have gone rapidly and yet so many then living are now gone.

June 23. They call us at 4:15 a.m. But before we can get started Mother Miller passes away. Not unexpectedly—yet not expected just now.

December 29. A day off to play with the grandchildren. A little rest!

1932

March 22. Dr. Holl reports his visit to Chicago. Students and all are pleased over entrance to the North Central Association.

March 23. Dr. Cordier and others present the candidacy of Professor J. R. Schutz for nomination to Congress.

1938

November 3. Work all day [at Elgin]. Meeting closed at 3 p.m., but I am too tired to leave Elgin.

1939

March 3. A strenuous week of Board Meetings. Completed about 10. To Chicago and Warsaw. Home at 8:00.

1936

April 4. I work all day in office and until midnight. Have headache in evening.

April 5. To Huntington in A.M. To Marion Baptist Church in P.M. Terrible headache. Call Dr. Beaman.

April 6. To Chicago on morning train. Sat by Paul Trebelcock all day. I am sick. Terrible night at New Weston Hotel.

April 7. Can't sit longer for Trebelcock. Home and to Bluffton Clinic. All night in Wells Co. Hospital.

April 10. Home but no better.

April 14. To Bluffton. Dr. consents for me to go to Elgin.

April 15. To Elgin with Lorrell Eikenberry. Attend Board Meeting in P.M.

April 16. Board Meeting in A.M. Back home in P. M.

April 17. To Bluffton and arrange for operation. Give Commencement address at Argos High School.

April 18. To Bluffton—Wells Co. Hospital—operation. Don't remember much today. Mother with me. Mrs. Hackinjos, nurse.

April 25. Mother stays with me tonight.

1940

May 1. With J. O. I went to Richmond there I talked to Earlham College. Then we went to Dayton, saw N. Wine and to Gettysburg to see Ray Petersime.

May 2. Sciatica bother me more.

May 3. Left side numb. J. O. took me to Caylor Nickle Clinic and Hospital. . . .

May 4. I remain for a week. They call it peripheral paralysis.

May 5. While I do not have a special nurse I do have wonderful care.

May 6. This is a great hospital. I have many visitors. J. O. comes often.

May 10. I come home with J. O. Some better. Lowell Noffsinger takes much care of me.

May 12. A long Sunday. Many visitors.

May 13. Slowly recovering.

May 25. Directing Lowell in doing work about home. Not spending so much time at College.